EDUCATION

✚ RECLAIMING THE CHRISTIAN INTELLECTUAL TRADITION

David S. Dockery, series editor

CONSULTING EDITORS

Hunter Baker
Timothy George
Niel Nielson
Philip G. Ryken
Michael J. Wilkins
John D. Woodbridge

OTHER RCIT VOLUMES:

Art and Music, Paul Munson and Joshua Farris Drake

Christian Worldview, Philip G. Ryken

Ethics and Moral Reasoning, C. Ben Mitchell

The Great Tradition of Christian Thinking, David S. Dockery and Timothy George

History, Nathan A. Finn

The Liberal Arts, Gene C. Fant Jr.

Literature, Louis Markos

Media, Journalism, and Communication, Read Mercer Schuchardt

The Natural Sciences, John A. Bloom

Philosophy, David K. Naugle

Political Thought, Hunter Baker

Psychology, Stanton L. Jones

EDUCATION
A STUDENT'S GUIDE

Ted Newell

WHEATON, ILLINOIS

Trade paperback ISBN: 978-1-4335-5493-3
ePub ISBN: 978-1-4335-5496-4
PDF ISBN: 978-1-4335-5494-0
Mobipocket ISBN: 978-1-4335-5495-7

Library of Congress Cataloging-in-Publication Data

Names: Newell, Ted, author.
Title: Education : a student's guide / Ted Newell.
Description: Wheaton, Illinois : Crossway, [2019] | Series: Reclaiming the Christian intellectual tradition | Includes bibliographical references and index.
Identifiers: LCCN 2018013751 (print) | LCCN 2018044334 (ebook) | ISBN 9781433554940 (pdf) | ISBN 9781433554957 (mobi) | ISBN 9781433554964 (epub) | ISBN 9781433554933 (pbk.) | ISBN 9781433554964 (epub)
Subjects: LCSH: Christian education—Study and teaching. | Christian education—History.
Classification: LCC BV1471.3 (ebook) | LCC BV1471.3 .N485 2019 (print) | DDC 261.5—dc23
LC record available at https://lccn.loc.gov/2018013751

Crossway is a publishing ministry of Good News Publishers.

VP		29	28	27	26	25	24	23	22	21	20	19
15	14	13	12	11	10	9	8	7	6	5	4	3	2	1

CONTENTS

SERIES PREFACE

The Reclaiming the Christian Intellectual Tradition series is designed to provide an overview of the distinctive way the church has read the Bible, formulated doctrine, provided education, and engaged the culture. The contributors to this series all agree that personal faith and genuine Christian piety are essential for the life of Christ followers and for the church. These contributors also believe that helping others recognize the importance of serious thinking about God, Scripture, and the world needs a renewed emphasis at this time in order that the truth claims of the Christian faith can be passed along from one generation to the next. The study guides in this series will enable believers to see afresh how the Christian faith shapes how we live, how we think, how we write books, how we govern society, and how we relate to one another in our churches and social structures. The richness of the Christian intellectual tradition provides guidance for the complex challenges that believers face in this world.

This series is particularly designed for Christian students and others associated with college and university campuses, including faculty, staff, trustees, and other various constituents. The contributors to the series will explore how the Bible has been interpreted in the history of the church, as well as how theology has been formulated. They will ask: How does the Christian faith influence our understanding of culture, literature, philosophy, government, beauty, art, or work? How does the Christian intellectual tradition help us understand truth? How does the Christian intellectual tradition shape our approach to education? We believe that this series is not only timely but that it meets an important need, because the secular culture in which we now find ourselves is, at best, indifferent to the Christian faith, and the Christian world—at least in its more popular forms—tends to be confused about the beliefs, heritage, and tradition associated with the Christian faith.

At the heart of this work is the challenge to prepare a generation of Christians to think Christianly, to engage the academy and the culture, and to serve church and society. We believe that both the breadth and the depth of the Christian intellectual tradition need to be reclaimed, revitalized, renewed, and revived for us to carry this work forward. These study guides seek to provide a framework to help introduce students to the great tradition of Christian thinking, seeking to highlight its importance for understanding the world, its significance for serving both church and society, and its application for Christian thinking and learning. The series is a starting point for exploring important ideas and issues such as truth, meaning, beauty, and justice.

We trust that the series will help introduce readers to the apostles, church fathers, Reformers, philosophers, theologians, historians, and a wide variety of other significant thinkers. In addition to well-known leaders such as Clement, Origen, Augustine, Thomas Aquinas, Martin Luther, and Jonathan Edwards, readers will be pointed to William Wilberforce, G. K. Chesterton, T. S. Eliot, Dorothy Sayers, C. S. Lewis, Johann Sebastian Bach, Isaac Newton, Johannes Kepler, George Washington Carver, Elizabeth Fox-Genovese, Michael Polanyi, Henry Luke Orombi, and many others. In doing so, we hope to introduce those who throughout history have demonstrated that it is indeed possible to be serious about the life of the mind while simultaneously being deeply committed Christians.

These efforts to strengthen serious Christian thinking and scholarship will not be limited to the study of theology, scriptural interpretation, or philosophy, even though these areas provide the framework for understanding the Christian faith for all other areas of exploration. In order for us to reclaim and advance the Christian intellectual tradition, we must have some understanding of the tradition itself. The volumes in this series seek to explore this tradition and its application for our twenty-first-century world. Each volume contains a glossary, study questions, and a list of resources for further study, which we trust will provide helpful guidance for our readers.

I am deeply grateful to the series editorial committee: Timothy George, John Woodbridge, Michael Wilkins, Niel Nielson, Philip Ryken, and Hunter Baker. Each of these colleagues joins me in thanking our various contributors for their fine work. We all express our appreciation to Justin Taylor, Jill Carter, Allan Fisher, Lane Dennis, and the Crossway team for their enthusiastic support for this project. We offer the project with the hope that students will be helped, faculty and Christian leaders will be encouraged, institutions will be strengthened, churches will be built up, and, ultimately, that God will be glorified.

Soli Deo Gloria
David S. Dockery
Series Editor

1

THE POTENTIAL OF CHRISTIAN EDUCATION

When disciplined learning tells the Christian story in a fresh way, history has shown that vibrant expressions of faith result:

- In the 800s, organized learning in a Europe united under Charlemagne brought a time of confidence when Christian culture flowered.
- The 1100s renewal of learning seen in figures like Anselm and Bernard of Clairvaux led to the first universities.
- The 1400s revival of humanistic learning in northern Europe and diffusion of books from the movable-type printing press raised interest in what Scripture really taught. The next generation saw a widespread renewal of faith in Christ.
- John Wesley, the mid-eighteenth-century evangelist to Britain and America, maintained the gains of the Great Awakening for at least another century through Bible learning carried out in small groups called "classes."
- Denominations formed universities in the 1800s to train leaders for churches and society. University-based revivals brought urgency to the worldwide Christian movement.

Education can foster a wide renewal of the Christian story in our time and place. Initiatives in education can be a sign of Christian renewal, and feed it. Getting the story right changes people. Imaginations are fired. Believers reclaim a vision for evangelism, missions, church life, education, and family life.

This guide aims to introduce the academic field of education in a Christian perspective. It takes Christian education in the widest perspective possible. It discusses all types of disciplined learning—schools, universities, seminaries, local churches, parachurch organizations, youth ministries, and families.

Education has a strong claim as the very first Christian intellectual tradition. The apostles Paul, John, Peter, and others wrote documents for local churches in Corinth or Rome and elsewhere where individuals engaged in a battle of knowledge. The New Testament effort might be summed up in 2 Corinthians 10:5: "We demolish arguments and every pretension that sets itself up against the knowledge of God, and we take captive every thought to make it obedient to Christ" (NIV).

These chapters show how Christians accept a too-narrow understanding of education's work. The modern world dramatically narrows the range in which historic Christian beliefs are public knowledge. This guide shows how to reclaim a Christian intellectual tradition in education.

SIGNS OF LIFE, PORTENTS OF THE FUTURE

But first, a question: Does the Christian intellectual tradition of education really need to be reclaimed?

On the surface, Christian thinking about education is much in evidence. If academic writing about education indicates a Christian intellectual tradition, then publishers issue hundreds of new books, journal articles, and curricula every month. It would be impossible to attend all Christian academic, professional, or family conferences about education that are convened all over the world every week of the year, to say nothing about the dozens of education courses in seminaries and Christian universities and innumerable websites and podcasts. Christian education displays vibrant vital signs.

Imagine an alien investigator. Even if it limited its investigation of education to conservative Protestant or evangelical families, churches, youth ministries, parachurch organizations, schools, universities, and seminaries in the early 2000s, it would find a day-school movement of tens of thousands of schools on all continents, largely expanded since the 1960s, with dozens of curriculum publishers and two major associations.

It would find a homeschooling movement embracing nearly two million children in 2012 in the US (the largest homeschooling country) directed by books, curricula, and conferences.[1]

It would find a classical education movement for day schools and homeschools, with more curricula, blogs, and conferences.

It would find conservative Protestant or evangelical universities with published rationales for existence, along with professional journals and conferences, in addition to similar intellectual activity for Catholic universities and other faith groups. The process of confirming employment at an evangelical university often elicits a specific statement of Christian beliefs from the professor. Administrators scrutinize thousands of their statements about Christianity and education. Hundreds more professors teach church education to seminary or undergraduate students.

On secular university campuses, our alien would find student groups such as InterVarsity Christian Fellowship, Cru, and smaller groups—all teaching Christian beliefs to future leaders.

Neither would the alien find educational thinking absent in conservative churches. Sunday school materials plus mid-week and summer programming from Christian publishers would find a place in its survey. Parents would be seen absorbing programs from sources such as Focus on the Family and similar parachurch agencies. Church leaders would be noted as having the choice of offsite learning for leadership development conferences via worldwide satellite link.

Our alien might conclude that a Christian tradition of education is alive in thought and practice.

And yet . . .

---

[1] Jeremy Redford, Danielle Battle, and Stacey Bielick, "Homeschooling in the United States: 2012," November 2016, https://eric.ed.gov/?id=ED569947.

Sociological surveys since the late 1990s reveal that as few as 40 percent of American young adults who grew up in evangelical churches still attend services regularly. The phenomenon of low adult adherence is apparent in Canada, Australia, and Europe— across Western societies.

Moreover, the faith that young adults confess is different than that of their parents and of the historic declarations of Christian faith such as the Apostles' Creed. Researcher Christian Smith memorably tagged the new faith as "Moralistic, Therapeutic Deism," marked by five beliefs:

> First, a God exists who created and orders the world and watches over human life on earth. Second, God wants people to be good, nice, and fair to each other, as taught in the Bible and by most world religions. Third, the central goal of life is to be happy and to feel good about oneself. Fourth, God does not need to be particularly involved in one's life except when God is needed to resolve a problem. Fifth, good people go to heaven when they die.[2]

Smith and fellow researchers emphasize that teens and young adults function with the restricted faith that their parents model. The life-world of teens and young adults is not its own world; it is largely copied from older adults. Parents are gatekeepers for influences that shape their children up to their teen years. However, these key educators are competing in an ecology with mass media, peers, formal education, the legal environment, and churches. The social ecology expresses long and deep social trends.[3]

---

[2] Christian Smith and Patricia Snell, *Souls in Transition: The Religious and Spiritual Lives of Emerging Adults* (New York: Oxford University Press, 2009), 154–55.

[3] Christian Smith and Melinda Lundquist Denton, *Soul Searching: The Religious and Spiritual Lives of American Teenagers* (New York: Oxford University Press, 2005), 118–71; David Kinnaman, *You Lost Me: Why Young Christians Are Leaving Church . . . and Rethinking Faith*, International ed. (Grand Rapids, MI: Baker, 2011); James Penner, R. Harder, R. Hiemstra, E. Anderson, and B. Désorcy, "Hemorrhaging Faith: Why and When Canadian Young Adults Are Leaving, Staying and Returning to Church," Foundational Research Document Commissioned by EFC Youth and Young Adult Ministry Roundtable (Ottawa, Canada: Evangelical Fellowship of Canada, 2012); Mark McCrindle, "A Demographic Snapshot of Christianity and Church Attenders in Australia" (Bella Vista, NSW, Australia: McCrindle Research, April 18, 2014); Vern L. Bengtson, Norella M. Putney, and Susan Harris, *Families and Faith: How Religion Is Passed Down across Generations* (New York: Oxford University Press, 2013).

If education is the whole process of personal development, then the dismal news is that Christian education is in crisis. Despite the many evidences of intellectual activity that our alien surveyed, other factors are working against mature adherence to orthodox Christian faith. Reclaiming a Christian intellectual tradition in education is an urgent task.

DEFINING "EDUCATION"

Education can be defined as widely as "learning a culture." The meaning of the Latin term *educare* is "to educe, to draw out latent possibilities." While the metaphor focuses attention on individual development, education can encompass all learning that makes learners competent in a culture over a lifespan. The German word, *bildung*, means the wide-angle view of formation that educator John White simplifies as "upbringing."[4]

The nation of Israel long had to live as God's people in a pressurized environment where rewards came for conforming to the norm. After the destruction of Jerusalem and the exile of most Jews in 587 BC, Jewish life took root outside Palestine—from Odessa and Samarkand in the east to Spain in the west. Jews adopted a more-or-less deliberate strategy to maintain Jewish distinctiveness. They developed an institution for their unique worship and education. First attested in Egypt, synagogues seem to have started as houses of learning, two centuries before Christ. By the first century before Christ, synagogues hosted Sabbath worship. Through distinctive worship and study, Jewish communities resisted surrounding dominant cultures and maintained their faith and way of life.[5]

Basic beliefs sustain all cultures. Big-scale stories explain the world, human origins, and human destiny. A culture or subculture may tell its animating narrative explicitly. The animating narrative

---

[4] John White, *The Aims of Education Restated*, International Library of the Philosophy of Education, vol. 22 (London and Boston: Routledge & Kegan Paul, 1982), 5.
[5] Shaye J. D. Cohen, *From the Maccabees to the Mishnah*, 2nd ed. (Louisville, KY: Westminster/ John Knox Press, 2006), 99–118.

for Christians is, naturally, the Old and New Testaments. Sunday-by-Sunday, preaching explains and underlines the Christian animating narrative to its people. Over time, a culture's master narrative is its living tradition.

The apostles' metaphor for church life is *edification* (literally meaning "up-building"). It draws on the process of building a temple, course upon course of crafted stones. In the metaphor, the church is the new house of worship. This time, the house of God is a spiritual reality, and Spirit-formed persons are the crafted stones. Edification is not only for intellectual capacities. It imagines the lives of all individuals built into a collective faith expression that is true worship of God (Eph. 4:12, 16, 29; 1 Corinthians 14; 1 Thess. 5:11; 1 Pet. 2:5; cf. Ps. 28:5; Luke 6:48).

Not only is a big-scale story like the gospel told verbally. Four processes tell and retell the master narrative. These processes can be helpfully labeled as *Memory*, *Vision*, *Symbols*, and *Ethos*.[6]

- **Memory:** A community recalls and recasts its history or recent events in light of its master narrative.
- **Vision:** A community draws on its master narrative to lift up its Vision as a preferred future, a hope worth living for.
- **Symbols:** Symbols and rituals recapitulate the master narrative in which the society lives. Shared Symbols and rituals include and initiate new members of a community.
- **Ethos:** The animating narrative generates a way of life. An Ethos is a master narrative's right way of living.

A member of society is educated in the widest sense as she lives her society's tradition. By Memory, Vision, Symbols, and Ethos, she is led to participate in her culture.

Importantly, Memory, Vision, Symbols, and Ethos do not pass on a dead tradition. As leaders and teachers convey a society's experiences

---

[6] H. Fernhout, "Christian Schooling: Telling a World View Story," in *The Crumbling Walls of Certainty: Towards a Christian Critique of Postmodernity and Education*, ed. I. Lambert and S. Mitchell (Sydney, Australia: Centre for the Study of Australian Christianity, 1997), 75–96.

to the new generation, the young examine the history, question it, and push back. A tradition cannot be passively inherited. Cultural leaders, teachers, and parents adapt and reshape a society's Memory to make its cultural heritage fresh again. Memory shifts. The Vision may alter. Symbols and rituals acquire new coloring. The Ethos may shift. A living tradition prompts fresh expressions in art, politics, language, and every form of culture. Individuals may accept or reject the expressions and, with them, the animating narrative they embody. In short, the rising generation accepts and reshapes its tradition.

Renewed Christian education's content and disciplines can therefore play a major role in Christian renewal. Formal education is more than passing on propositions. Disciplined learning deliberately passes on key intellectual and moral knowledge, skills, and habits for the continued life of a society. Disciplined learning expresses Memory, Vision, Symbols, and Ethos in its content and processes.

STORY COMPETITION

Today, telling the Christian story over a flood of dissonant noise and activity takes determination. Church members who watch major sporting events or take in studio films absorb master narratives with values other than Christian ones. This means that compared to the flood of culturing inputs over the previous six days, a pastor's twenty-minute sermon struggles to form anyone in its image, even when accompanied by overhead slides or video segments.[7]

Animating narratives compete among civilizations. Decades ago, the political scientist Samuel Huntington raised the prospect of clashing civilizations. After the Cold War, Islam's story would compete with secular modern societies. When an Islamic group proposes a minaret to call its faithful to prayer in a Swiss canton, the competition of narratives is visible. Symbols clash.[8]

---

[7] Dwayne Huebner, "Can Theological Education Be Church Education?," *Union Seminary Quarterly Review* 47 (1993): 23–38; Michael Warren, "Religious Formation in the Context of Social Formation," in *Critical Perspectives on Christian Education: A Reader on the Aims, Principles and Philosophy of Christian Education*, ed. Jeff Astley and Leslie J. Francis (Leominster, UK: Gracewing, 1994), 202–14.
[8] Samuel P. Huntington, "The Clash of Civilizations?," *Foreign Affairs* 72, no. 3 (Summer 1993): 22–49.

Animating narratives compete inside civilizations too. Rival accounts of history, rival preferred futures, proposed new Symbols of a society, and alternative ethoses compete with each other. Influential philosopher Alasdair MacIntyre points out that a tradition is best understood as a long argument about its master story and identity.[9] A culture is not usually monolithic; it includes dissonant voices in its stream. In the way that advertisement competes with advertisement and brand competes with brand, national political parties and interest groups tell rival stories of their nation's past, present, and future. Teachers in schools compete with undisciplined "teachers" who teach on small screens, twenty-four hours a day. Rival storytellers challenge Christian education in families, churches, schools, and universities.

Perhaps nowhere is story competition clearer than from long-term studies of how the media cultivates values. Communications researcher George Gerbner and researchers at the University of Pennsylvania tracked thousands of characters in network television shows over decades from the 1960s onward.[10] Gerbner's studies demonstrated that heavy viewers tend to absorb mass-media attitudes about race, economic status, occupations, and gender. Heavy television and media viewers tended to adopt and follow the ideas from their main source of information. Viewers who were less influenced relied on a wider variety of information sources.

Mass-media stories cultivate a skewed way of seeing the world. This sounds less revolutionary than it is. Gerbner saw that new-world technologies pass on a worldview. Media repeats its stories like villages repeated folktales in premodern Europe, traditional African societies, and elsewhere.

Positively, schools can become sites of resistance or renewal exactly because they are not a society's only educators. Take, for

---

[9] Alasdair C. MacIntyre, "Epistemological Crises, Dramatic Narrative, and the Philosophy of Science," in *Paradigms and Revolutions: Appraisals and Applications of Thomas Kuhn's Philosophy of Science*, ed. Gary Gutting (South Bend, IN: University of Notre Dame Press, 1974), 54–74.

[10] George Gerbner, "Telling Stories in the Information Age," in *Information and Behavior*, ed. Brent D. Ruben (New Brunswick, NJ and Oxford: Transaction Publishers, 1987), 3–12; *Against the Mainstream: The Selected Works of George Gerbner*, ed. M. Morgan (New York: Peter Lang, 2002).

example, the value our society puts on competitiveness over cooperation. Many agencies inculcate competitiveness. Even if public schools were to reform the hidden curriculum of competition, families and institutions such as Scouting or organized sports would continue to teach competitive expectations, beliefs, and behaviors. On the other hand, schools could raise public awareness through specific programs to resist the hidden curriculum of competition.

Because host or majority cultures tell their story all the time in many ways, a subculture must find ways to keep its own story alive before adherents and initiates. Like the Jewish diaspora in Hellenistic culture, a subculture can learn to push back against stories that undermine its own narrative. To resist rivals, the Christian story must be sustained verbally. Equally, Christians must enact fresh ways of living their animating narrative.

WIDE-ANGLE EDUCATION AND FORMAL EDUCATION

Formal education or ordered learning is one component of the broad process of cultural reproduction. Formal education is not a similar task across cultures, because each varies with its choice of aims. Schooling's content imparts a culture's habits and disciplines through its procedures and rituals. *Curriculum* is a Latin term for a circular course, as in a racecourse. A repeated course includes predictable obstacles that learners must overcome.

Educators point out three forms of curriculum: (1) the stated or official written curriculum; (2) a null curriculum; and (3) a hidden curriculum. Through an educational system's disciplines, ordered learning passes on selected key aptitudes so a new generation maintains the sponsor generation's ways of life and belief.

WRITTEN CURRICULUM

The first curriculum is the *written* curriculum. It describes the formal content of schooling. In modern Western publicly funded education, government departments of education or other similar sponsors list topics and outcomes for each grade and subject—for example, tenth grade mathematics at college preparatory level. Teachers teach and test prescribed topics. Textbooks, films, or computer programs also form part of the stated curriculum.

Choices of formal knowledge are political, because the official curriculum teaches a way of life, an Ethos. Not only education professionals but also elected officials, parents, the public, and special-interest groups influence the selection process. Knowledge in the official curriculum is privileged knowledge that reflects the outcome of a struggle for a culture's Memory and Vision. What one group of constituents values and wishes to have preserved and enhanced, another party may see as backward-tending and in need of elimination for a bright future. A written curriculum's approval symbolizes the victory of one interpretation of a culture.

NULL CURRICULUM

The second curriculum is the *null curriculum*. Curriculum making forces choices. Selections on content must be made. All knowledge cannot be packed into even twelve or thirteen years of formal schooling. Society deems some knowledge not important enough to merit inclusion. Yet silence in schools about a particular area of knowledge indicates the relative value that is placed upon that knowledge by the collective. Such silencing comes through a political process, from oversight, or from collective amnesia. The null curriculum is the content that is not covered.

A strong case can be made that the largest null curriculum in public schooling and universities today is religion. Where taught, religion is described from outside. Its concern for meaning in life is almost entirely ignored.[11]

---

[11] Elliot W. Eisner, *The Educational Imagination: On the Design and Evaluation of School Programs*, 3rd ed. (Upper Saddle River, NJ: Merrill Prentice Hall, 1994); Warren A. Nord, *Religion and American Education: Rethinking a National Dilemma* (Chapel Hill: UNC Press, 1995); W. A. Nord, *Does*

HIDDEN CURRICULUM

The third curriculum is the *hidden curriculum*. The term refers to the "unofficial rules, routines, and structures of schools through which students learn behaviors, values, beliefs, and attitudes." Teachers and pupils come to school with expectations. An established social setting like a classroom has inherited norms. For example, teachers must receive respect. Students must defer to teacher authority and to teacher definitions of knowledge and what makes "success" in school. Students or pupils learn the norms from school administrators, other students, and most of all from their teachers who impose discipline and who possess power to assess classroom performance. "Hidden" does not imply an intention to hide or to deceive anyone; it only suggests that the procedures and intentions are mostly undocumented. The third curriculum is hidden because "elements . . . do not appear in schools' written goals, formal lesson plans, or learning objectives."[12] Close attention to the way that modern-era schools squeeze students into their mold shows that any schooling seeks a preferred outcome in students' lives.

The education scholar Philip Jackson, publishing in the 1960s, showed that schools taught students to defer to higher authority. Later studies noticed that few students move from low socioeconomic schools to high social standing. The result is that mass education tends to reproduce the existing social structure. Studies in the 1980s and 1990s went on to emphasize that some student subcultures resist fitting into a majority mold. Students are not merely like clay, receiving shape from the system, but are active "agents" who work out responses to dominant ways. For example, rappers resist a system that does not suit them. However, the most recent wave sees schooling as an initiation ritual where repeated

God Make a Difference?: Taking Religion Seriously in Our Schools and Universities (New York: Oxford University Press, 2010), 87–107.
[12] Alan Skelton, "Studying Hidden Curricula: Developing a Perspective in the Light of Postmodern Insights," *Curriculum Studies* 5, no. 2 (1997): 188.

procedures, rewards, and penalties—or reactions to them—serve to slot students into society's structures.[13]

Education happens in a field of symbolic actions that go back for generations. Schooling is an enterprise with a history. Erasing and replacing deep-seated understandings is difficult. "Good education" comes less from any rational reconstruction than from our interpretation of experience—our history. What makes a "good education" is unlikely to be shifted by any top-down rationale. Efficiency-promoting proposals for education are likely to miss the way human beings come to know themselves.[14]

Peter McLaren, a researcher, sat in a ninth grade classroom in a Catholic school in Toronto, Canada, for months in the 1980s. He documented speech and behaviors of mainly immigrant Portuguese Catholic students and their teachers. He tabulated patterns like an anthropologist might study a Papua New Guinea language group to make a "thick interpretation." McLaren showed that the school's regular patterns of compliance reproduced students as future workers. The school achieved its disciplines by sheer repetition. Though the school sincerely presented the Catholic faith and accorded it formal authority, religion functioned to make students acquiesce to their worker fate. Teachers came to expect from students what their peers and administrators expected. They marginalized student experiences from the "street," seeing them as threats. Mr. Keating (of the film *Dead Poets Society*) and mold-breaking teachers in real life are exceptions to the

[13] Philip W. Jackson, *Life in Classrooms* (New York: Holt, Rinehart and Winston, 1968); Jean Anyon, "Social Class and School Knowledge," *Curriculum Inquiry* 11, no. 1 (1981): 3–42; Michael W. Apple and Philip Wexler, "Cultural Capital and Educational Transmissions: An Essay on Basil Bernstein, Class, Codes and Control: Vol. III—Towards a Theory of Educational Transmissions," *Educational Theory* 28, no. 1 (1978): 34–43; Michael W. Apple and Nancy R. King, "What Do Schools Teach?," *Curriculum Inquiry* 6, no. 4 (1977): 341; David B. Tyack, *The One Best System: A History of American Urban Education* (Cambridge, MA: Harvard University Press, 1974); Stuart Hall, "Encoding, Decoding," in *The Cultural Studies Reader*, ed. Simon During, 2nd ed. (London: Routledge, 1999), 90–103; Stuart Hall and Tony Jefferson, eds., *Resistance through Rituals: Youth Subcultures in Post-War Britain*, 2nd ed. (London and New York: Routledge, 2006).

[14] Jackson, *Life in Classrooms*; Edward Farley, "The Tragic Dilemma of Church Education," in *Caring for the Commonweal: Education for Religious and Public Life*, ed. Parker J. Palmer, Barbara G. Wheeler, and Robert W. Lynn (Atlanta: Mercer University Press, 1990), 131.

conformity-producing norm. Hidden curriculum has extensive and subtle power.[15]

Hidden curriculum studies demonstrate how schooling imparts a preferred image of human beings. Feminist critics long ago noted that schools overlook women's lives, experiences, and activities. Schools form their ideal of future roles from occupations for which men have traditionally been suited. Moreover, when schools do not acknowledge the traits, dispositions, or skills traditionally associated with reproductive processes, they harm both sexes. Public schools reproduce modern-era people. The worldwide spread of modern Western schooling gives the impression of a "one best way," but modern-era public schools shape students to fit a pluralistic, democratic, capitalist, individualistic, and egalitarian culture.[16]

Hidden curriculum is schooling's cultivating process. Learning's disciplines—its procedures, rewards, and punishments—lead students to live a story. Educational procedures amount to rituals through which students project their futures as members of society. The hidden curriculum is what stays with a person when the formal lessons have been forgotten.

> Education is an undertaking in a community whose aims is the disciplining of various modes of interpretation already occurring in the life of that community.[17]

This strange quote is from Edward Farley. He speaks of education as learning to interpret. Disciplined learning is about making meaning, about fitting new knowledge into patterns, about trying to see things whole.

---

[15] Peter McLaren, *Schooling as a Ritual Performance: Toward a Political Economy of Educational Symbols and Gestures* (Lanham, MD: Rowman & Littlefield, 1999).

[16] Jane Roland Martin, "What Should We Do with a Hidden Curriculum When We Find One?," in *Changing the Educational Landscape: Philosophy, Women, and Curriculum* (New York and London: Routledge, 1994), 154–69.

[17] Edward Farley, "The Tragic Dilemma of Church Education," in *Caring for the Commonwealth: Education for Religious and Public Life*, ed. Parker J. Palmer, Barbara G. Wheeler, and Robert W. Lynn (Atlanta: Mercer University Press, 1990), 131–2.

Written, null, and hidden curricula together aim for a distinctive formation. Across cultures, schooling's three curricula shape students for a preferred image or ideal. Disciplined learning is an integrated process of cultivating a desired kind of human being.

RECLAIMING CHRISTIAN EDUCATION

This guide surveys education as a single field. Different vantage points on the field are possible. *Historical*, *philosophical*, or *social theory* lenses yield perspectives on the discipline of education.

When *philosophy* provides the lens, successive understandings of knowledge make textbook models of education. The models are entitled "realism," "perennialism," or "student-centered." These labels appear tidy and accurate. Without more historical context, though, it is hard to understand why one philosophy fades, only to be replaced by another. In contrast, *anthropology* sees education as a function of cultural transmission. The lens of *psychology* underlines different learning theories. These underpin different ways individuals are taught. Each lens gives a helpful but partial picture.

Reclaiming a Christian intellectual tradition in education needs more than a restatement of philosophy or theology. The bigger picture is that a philosophy of education or a learning psychology makes sense within its cultural setting in a particular time.

Education is a practice. It tells a story by passing on a tradition. Agencies of education such as family, school, or mass media form an *ecology* of cultural transmission. *Paradigm thinking* has been especially helpful for fields where Christian beliefs are expressed as practices. Pioneering philosopher of science Thomas Kuhn brought paradigm thinking to the history of science; he leads us to see different education ecologies as alternative paradigms. The theologian Hans Küng used paradigms to make sense of eras in church history, missions scholar David Bosch explained paradigms of Christian mission, and the religious educator Mary Boys used paradigms to find the basic contours of Protestant and Catholic religious education. Theologian and philosopher Harry Fernhout's story model, with its elements of Memory, Vision, Symbols, and Ethos, sees education ecologies as paradigms.[18]

This guide profiles five distinct paradigms or traditions of formation to show how Christians thought about education in different eras throughout history. Christian education is an enterprise with two thousand years of history. Selected paradigms derive from Jesus's ministry, from the Greco-Roman city-state, from cloistered settings, from the era of Scientific Revolution, and from the subjectivist reply to science. Understanding ways of education in their historical context enables us to see how Christian educators can reclaim their task.

---

[18] Thomas S. Kuhn, *The Structure of Scientific Revolutions: 50th Anniversary Edition*, Fourth ed. (Chicago and London: University of Chicago Press, 2012); Hans Küng and David Tracy, *Paradigm Change in Theology* (New York: Crossroad, 1989); David J. Bosch, *Transforming Mission: Paradigm Shifts in Theology of Mission*, vol. 16, American Society of Missiology series (Maryknoll, NY: Orbis, 1991); Mary C. Boys, *Educating in Faith: Maps and Visions* (New York: Harper & Row, 1989).

2

JESUS'S EDUCATION

AD 29-33

Teaching is deeply rooted in the scriptural record. God directly taught the first human pair (Gen. 1:28; 2:16–17). God's Spirit taught Israel during their Sinai desert sojourn (Neh. 9:14, 20). When the Creator teaches humans to imitate his ways, his followers' lives are blessed (Ps. 94:10, 12; e.g., 25:4–5, 8–10). God will teach the nations that will stream to Israel's holy city at the end of the age, according to the prophets Isaiah and Micah (Isa. 2:3; Mic. 4:2).[1]

Scripture speaks of God as teacher of Israel in a broader way than explicit teaching. Because God controls all events in history, events in time are meant to teach Israel heartfelt allegiance. This appears clearly in Joseph's interpretation of his trials (Gen. 50:15–21), in Moses's prediction of the nation's future (Deuteronomy 30), and in the prophets (Isa. 2:1–5; Jer. 33:1–26; Ezek. 37:1–14; Dan. 12:1–13). Hosea's prophecy promises restoration: "I will heal their apostasy; I will love them freely" (Hos. 14:4). If education is the process of shaping people by cognitive content inculcated by bodily disciplines or routines, then Israel's God is the nation's educator.

Human beings share God's educating work. God charges Moses to teach the next generation—critically important for

---

[1] Donn F. Morgan, "Education," ed. David Noel Freedman, Astrid B. Beck, and Allen C. Myers, *Eerdmans Dictionary of the Bible* (Grand Rapids, MI: Eerdmans, 2000).

Israel's continued faithfulness (Deut. 6:1–12; Ps. 78:1–8). Paul the apostle passes on patterns of belief and behavior that he himself received from others (2 Thess. 2:15; also Col. 1:28; 1 Tim. 2:7).

WHAT KIND OF TEACHER IS JESUS?

The documents describing Jesus's career—the four Gospels—make clear that he was a teacher. He proclaimed, and he instructed; the New Testament makes little distinction between these two activities. In dozens of instances, his contemporaries referred to him as "teacher" or a related term such as "rabbi," and he accepted the description (Mark 10:17–18; John 13:13).[2]

Writers who compare Jesus's teaching to a Western schooling model of education tend to approve of all his techniques. Educator H. H. Horne's *Jesus, the Master Teacher* "discusses every conceivable personal and pedagogical trait, judging Jesus to be highly accomplished on every item." More recently, Roy Zuck advises church educators to adopt Jesus's manner of picturesque expressions or, more plainly, to use his storytelling approach. These writers apply ancient techniques directly to a modern setting.[3]

Jesus was (and is) an unusual teacher. Even those who received special instruction—the twelve disciples—were confused at times (e.g., Mark 8:15–16; John 6:5–9; Acts 1:6). In Matthew 13, Israel appeared to have decided against Jesus. The disciples asked Jesus why he taught without clear meaning (v. 10). He replied, in effect, that the hearers had no right to know. He said he used parables to veil the truth.

Recent scholars seek to understand Jesus in his historical context. Some take the Hellenistic culture of the Roman Empire

---

[2] J. Stanley Glen, *The Recovery of the Teaching Ministry* (Philadelphia, PA: Westminster Press, 1960); Robert C. Worley, *Preaching and Teaching in the Earliest Church* (Philadelphia, PA: Westminster Press, 1967).

[3] J. T. Dillon, "The Effectiveness of Jesus as a Teacher," *Lumen Vitae* 36, no. 2 (1981): 156; *Jesus as a Teacher: A Multidisciplinary Case Study* (Bethesda, MD: International Scholars Publications, 1995); Herman H. Horne, *Jesus, the Master Teacher* (New York: Association Press, 1920); R. B. Zuck, *Teaching as Jesus Taught* (Grand Rapids, MI: Baker, 1995).

as the appropriate frame. Philosophical teachers in the Hellenistic context moved about from place to place. Accordingly, Jesus has been cast as a Cynic philosopher, a magician, or a spirit-possessed sage.[4]

How Jesus understood himself in his context is essential background to understand his behavior. Many scholars in the current "third wave" of Jesus studies accept Second-Temple Judaism in Palestine as the most relevant context. They see that Jesus taught a dissenting view of Israel's covenant with her God. Jesus's unusual manner of teaching gains a clear rationale once viewed through his understanding of his mission.[5]

TAUGHT WITH PARABLES

Jesus taught in the tradition of a wisdom teacher in Israel. He rarely used scholarly or technical language. He employed wisdom sayings, or *mashalim*—including puns, similes, metaphors, and proverbs sometimes in extended discourses. None of his techniques were unknown in the culture, and he used them with proficiency. Parables were already recorded in the Old Testament book of Judges as well as during King David's reign (Judg. 9:8–15; 2 Sam. 12:1–4). First-century religious leaders also employed them.[6]

Parables were Jesus's characteristic teaching technique for his provocative, symbol-redefining, dangerous mission. First, their oblique way of presenting truth was (and is) difficult to resist. Second, their storytelling form invites hearers to identity themselves in the narrative and to implicate themselves in their response. Third, they fulfill scriptural predictions of Israel's lack of response. And

---

[4] Craig A. Evans, *Fabricating Jesus: How Modern Scholars Distort the Gospels* (InterVarsity Press, 2006).

[5] N. T. Wright, *The New Testament and the People of God*, vol. 1, Christian Origins and the Question of God (London and Minneapolis: SPCK and Fortress, 1992), 76–77.

[6] Pheme Perkins, *Jesus as Teacher* (Cambridge: Cambridge University Press, 1990), 38; Gary M. Burge, Lynn H. Cohick, and Gene L. Green, *The New Testament in Antiquity: A Survey of the New Testament within Its Cultural Context* (New York: Harper Collins, 2010), 152.

finally, Jesus prevented early termination of his mission through these opaque stories.[7]

Second-Temple Jews understood their cultural Symbols and rituals to reflect reality as God had ordained it. Temple, land, Torah, and racial identity symbolically reiterated Israel's God-directed history. In worship and festivals, particularly Sabbath and Passover, Israel replayed its animating narrative each year. Jesus's parabolic teachings and parabolical actions defied dominant understanding of the day.

In Matthew 12:9–14, for instance, Jesus healed on the Sabbath. On a surface reading, Jesus's generous act brought on legal wrangling. His restoration of a withered hand violated the contemporary understanding of Torah. But a breach of legality was not the only problem. If it were, remedies were available to the penitent. However, Jesus intensified the offense by asserting his sovereignty over the Sabbath. In the way that King David's God-given mission overrode the normal application of the law (1 Sam. 21:1–9), so Jesus's God-given mission overrode the law. Jesus validated his claim with Scripture. The healing itself indicated the complicity of a supernatural power. No wonder the reaction from the guardians of the nation was that Jesus must die (Matt. 12:14).

How Jewish contemporaries understood Jesus also enables modern readers to grasp their reactions to him. For example, why did the high priest tear his robes at Jesus's trial (Matt. 26:65)? Jesus said that the high priest would see the Son of Man seated at the right hand of Power and coming on the clouds of heaven. While "seated on the right hand" and "coming on the clouds" appear to contradict each other, Second-Temple Jews knew exactly what Jesus was claiming. "Right hand" refers to Psalm 110:1, generally understood to predict the Messiah. "Coming on the clouds of

---

[7] Perkins, *Jesus as Teacher*, 38; Burge, Cohick, and Green, *The New Testament in Antiquity*, 152; Jack Sammons, "Parables and Pedagogy," in *Gladly Learn, Gladly Teach: Living Out One's Calling in the Twenty-First Century Academy*, ed. J. M. Dunaway (Macon, GA: Mercer University Press, 2005), 46–66.

heaven" refers to Daniel 7:9—the return of God's chariot throne. Jesus claims to be the human being of Daniel 7:13, the Son of God, and the expected Messiah in one breath. Jesus thus asserted that he would sit on God's throne and judge his accusers. Israel's most basic affirmation was the Shema of Deuteronomy 6: God is one. Jesus's language is thus highly charged. The high priest, refusing Jesus's affirmation, tore his clothes at the apparent blasphemy.[8]

TAUGHT WITH CULTURAL TEXTS

Jesus was an authoritative teacher who challenged his society's leadership from their own national texts. Modern-era parallels include Martin Luther King Jr., who challenged America through biblical narrative and the Declaration of Independence; Nelson Mandela challenged white South Africa; or Mohandas Gandhi, who challenged Great Britain. In each example, a minority's determined non-violence dared a Christian society to harm innocent fellows. Like these modern-era leaders who were inspired by him, Jesus taught that defying majority understandings means living the way of the cross. His disciples could expect that offense, pain, and even death would accompany the Messiah's cause.

TAUGHT THROUGH SYMBOLISM AND EVENTS

Jesus's symbolic acts teach a new reign of God. Nearly everything Jesus did educated his disciples about his new world order. He selected precisely twelve leading disciples. He healed untouchables such as blind persons, lepers, and an unclean female with an incurable flow of blood. He fed five thousand in a desert area with bread. He inverted the relationship of master and servant by washing his disciples' feet. Finally, he remade the traditional, divinely established festival of Passover to center on himself. Jesus's actions

---

[8] C. A. Evans, "What Did Jesus Do?," in *Jesus Under Fire: Modern Scholarship Reinvents the Historical Jesus* (Grand Rapids, MI: Zondervan, 1995), 110–11; "The Jesus of History and the Christ of Faith: Toward Jewish-Christian Dialogue," in *Who Was Jesus? A Jewish-Christian Dialogue*, ed. Paul Copan and C. A. Evans (Louisville, KY: Westminster John Knox Press, 2001), 63–66.

illustrated his understanding of the generous reign of God centered on himself. Jesus was always at the task of challenging and re-interpreting the dominant worldview. His actions were remembered and recorded precisely to instruct a new generation. Jesus knew that teaching could not be only verbal if disciples are going to absorb it. He taught didactically at times. However, he was as much or more a teacher through his embodied statements and actions, which make sense in a specific context.

As with Israel, God's direction of history made the disciples' education holistic, even existential. Israel's discontent after the daily miracle of food in the desert gave an opportunity for correction (Numbers 11; Psalm 95). In Mark 6, Jesus's disciples similarly saw five thousand men fed, with twelve baskets left over (vv. 43–44). In Mark 8, Jesus again fed about four thousand people (v. 9). This time, seven baskets were left over. Thus, the disciples revisited events that had already occurred in Mark 6. After the second demonstration of power, Jesus expressly asked them why their trust remained weak (Mark 8:14–21). Like Israel, the disciples learned from providential events.[9]

JESUS AS MASTER

How did Jesus's personality teach the disciples? This is a strange question until one remembers the personal impact that an outstanding teacher can have on a student. Learning includes more than testable, reproducible content. For example, in the 1987 film *Babette's Feast*, the revered late pastor left an immense but stern impression on his daughters, who were left as heads of his religious commune.[10] What a departed master did and said are cherished memories that shape a community's Ethos. Similarly, Jesus had

[9] Walter Wink, "The Education of the Apostles: Mark's View of Human Transformation," *Religious Education* 83, no. 2 (1988): 277–90; Mary Ann Tolbert, "How the Gospel of Mark Builds Character," *Interpretation: A Journal of Bible & Theology* 47, no. 4 (October 1993): 347; J. Ted Blakley, "Incomprehension or Resistance?: The Markan Disciples and the Narrative Logic of Mark 4:1—8:30" (University of St. Andrews, 2008).

[10] Gabriel Axel, *Babette's Feast* (Irvington, NY: The Criterion Collection, 2013).

a marked impact on his disciples: Temple leaders attributed the disciples' boldness and confident use of Scripture to the fact that they had been with Jesus (Acts 4:11–13). According to the Gospels, Jesus their teacher worked miracles. He healed a person blind from birth (John 9); performed dozens of healings; fed five thousand men, besides others (Matt. 14:13–21; Mark 6:30–44; Luke 9:10–17; John 6:1–15); walked on water (Matt. 14:22–33; John 6:16–21); and restored dead persons to life on several occasions (Matt. 9:18–26; Mark 5:21–43; Luke 7:11–17; John 11:38–44). Profound personal formation came from sharing life with such a master.

Any successful teaching passes on something of the teacher's personality. Wach contrasted the student/teacher relationship with the more intense master/disciple one. He stated that his concern was not with the specific content of the teachings proclaimed by the exalted master but with the meaning and value of the master's life, the "existence" of the master.[11] Seven decades later, responders believe he contrasted the teaching of subject matter and personal influence too sharply. They noted, "Our appreciation of intellectual originality is best taught in personalized teaching relationships." Even professors in academic settings relay themselves to students in lecturing, marking assignments, and personal conversations during office hours.[12]

Similarly, since knowing God means to be in relationship with God, it follows that followers must form a personal relationship with Jesus as master. Israel's God declares that "the earth will be filled with the knowledge of the glory of the LORD, as the waters cover the sea" (Hab. 2:14). Obviously, the knowledge will not be superficial. no prophet imagines that knowing the bare fact of God's existence is real knowledge. When Scripture refers to "no knowledge of God in the land," it means no practical obedience, no loyalty, no faithfulness

---

[11] Joachim Wach, "Master and Disciple: Two Religio-Sociological Studies," *The Journal of Religion* 42, no. 1 (1962): 6.

[12] Frederick M. Denny, Margaret R. Miles, Charles Hallisey, and Earle H. Waugh, "Joachim Wach's 'Master and Disciple' Revisited: A Contemporary Symposium," *Teaching Theology & Religion* 1, no. 1 (February 1, 1998): 17.

to God (Hos. 4:1; 6:6). The Old Testament's verb for *knowing* is also used to describe sexual intercourse. Adam "knew" his wife (Gen. 4:1; 1 Kings 1:4). "To know" in Scriptural context means truly personal knowledge.

God's love is his motive for educating his people. When God instructs Israel in his ways at Mount Sinai, his first commandment is loyalty: "I am the LORD your God, who brought you out of the land of Egypt" (Ex. 20:2). God freely chose Israel and entered a marriage-like covenant with the nation. The greatest instruction, "You shall love the LORD your God with all your heart . . ." (Deut. 6:5) is not forcing love. It is urging loyalty in return for God's loyalty. Therefore, Israel should desire education out of a heart for God.[13]

The ancients were more deeply aware than moderns that personal knowledge has shaping power. An influential strand of educational thinking since 1900 has sought to write curricula that is "teacher proof." But classical Greek education from Homer onward relied on mentors who could cultivate the virtues of a warrior. According to Plato, youths who admired an older philosophic exemplar could develop philosophical capacities.[14]

Modern settings still recognize the educating power of personality, at least sometimes. In 1871, US President James Garfield famously commended a college president of deep character: "Give me a log hut, with only a simple bench, Mark Hopkins on one end and I on the other, and you may have all the buildings, apparatus, and libraries without him." Philosophy of science since the mid-twentieth century allows for a personal knowledge that cannot be put into words. The philosopher Ludwig Wittgenstein likened teaching to a master/apprentice relationship where students observe to learn a craft. A craftsman may possess tacit knowledge that may be shown but not spoken. Scientists' ways of seeing rely on tacit knowledge. Teacher-proof learning is thus impersonal learn-

---

[13] Hanan A. Alexander, "God as Teacher: Jewish Reflections on a Theology of Pedagogy," *Journal of Beliefs and Values* 22 (April 1, 2001): 5–17.

[14] Plato, *Plato's Symposium*, trans. Seth Benardete (Chicago: University of Chicago Press, 1993).

ing. Teachers cannot be programmed like a computer. Their skill is practical, involving some of the attributes of a dance instructor or workshop instructor—"thinking on your feet" and "keeping your wits about you."[15]

Personal knowledge is at the heart of the Christian tradition of education. Luke Timothy Johnson, a New Testament scholar, reacts against academic teaching about Jesus. For Johnson, affirming Jesus's resurrection as historical event means also teaching that he is still alive.

> What we learn about Jesus must include what we can continue to learn from him. It is better to speak of "learning Jesus," rather than of "knowing Jesus," because we are concerned with a process rather than a product. Education that considers the Trinity of God the Father, God the Son, and God the Holy Spirit must include the implications for living. In a trinitarian way of seeing, bare knowledge is not whole knowledge.[16]

A teacher's personality invites students into a way of being in the world. The way of being can be an academic way stemming from Greek classicism. A teacher can also model a modern technical, rational, scientific way of being. Alternatively, Christian teachers can symbolize the kingdom to come in their own persons, so students catch the Christian animating narrative. Educator Parker Palmer urges a community of learning where teachers display the significance of their subject for a life—where they make it real. Imagine both students and teacher sitting around the subject that forms the center of their lives together. Teaching via practices that

---

[15] "Mark Hopkins," *Britannica Online Encyclopedia*, accessed May 19, 2017, https://www.britannica.com/print/article/271551; Nicholas C. Burbules, "Tacit Teaching," *Educational Philosophy & Theory* 40, no. 5 (September 2008): 666–77; Bryan R. Warnick, "How Do We Learn from the Lives of Others?," *Philosophy of Education Archive*, 2006, 367–75; Max Van Manen, "Pedagogy, Virtue, and Narrative Identity in Teaching," *Curriculum Inquiry* 24, no. 2 (1994): 135–70; "On the Epistemology of Reflective Practice," *Teachers and Teaching: Theory and Practice* 1, no. 1 (1995): 33–50; Donald A. Schön, *The Reflective Practitioner: How Professionals Think in Action* (New York: Basic Books, 1983), 54.
[16] Luke Timothy Johnson, *Living Jesus: Learning the Heart of the Gospel* (New York: HarperCollins, 2000), 56–76.

are consistent with Christian faith matches verbal profession with personal witness for a greater impact.[17]

SUMMARY OF JESUS'S EDUCATION

Jesus revolutionized Israel's tradition. He understood Israel's history from Abraham through Exile to Second Temple and that it all was to center on himself, God's promised Savior-King. In him the new era dawned. When John the Baptist's questioned, "Are you the one who is to come, or shall we look for another?" Jesus answered, "Go and tell John what you hear and see: the blind receive their sight and the lame walk, lepers are cleansed and the deaf hear, and the dead are raised up, and the poor have good news preached to them" (Matt. 11:2–5). In his proclamation and practice of the kingdom of God, the prophecies and promises of the age to come began to be reality.

- **Memory** was reworked.
- Jesus's **Vision** was (and is) the King returned and the kingdom promises fully realized.
- In line with the clarified cultural Memory and Vision, Jesus remade Israel's cultural **Symbols** and rituals. He reenacted the exodus and Passover to center on his actions. The Sermon on the Mount was a redemptive version of Moses's speech from Mount Sinai. Choosing the twelve disciples was choosing twelve new elders to lead a new Israel. Jesus made the traditions over in his image.
- Jesus's **Ethos** was (and is) his messianic reign activated in the lives of his followers. Every old practice must be questioned and renewed after the advent of Jesus the Messiah.

Jesus renewed education. Teaching the kingdom was far more than a set of propositions. Jesus did more than teach; he fully educated his disciples. The result was leaders who were able to pick up his countercultural movement after his resurrection and ascension.

---

[17] Parker J. Palmer, *The Courage to Teach: Exploring the Inner Landscape of a Teacher's Life*, 1st ed. (San Francisco: Jossey-Bass, 1997).

Early critics noted that Peter and John were adept at scriptural interpretation. Though uneducated by contemporary standards, they had been "companions of Jesus" (Acts 4:13 NRSV). Jesus accomplished their education as they followed him and learned to interpret his countercultural practices. The setting was life with the Master; its content was Scripture brought to life by submitting to the discipline of his mentorship.

Jesus's pedagogy of his person challenges any model that minimizes the work of teaching. The figure of the teacher in present-day classrooms models how living looks in a scientifically organized society. The teacher is also a persistent human figure in education, who comes alongside learners to explain and encourage. Jesus's example makes the teacher central in any education that would be called Christian.[18]

---

[18] J. M. Lee, *The Shape of Religious Instruction: A Social-Science Approach* (Birmingham, AL: Religious Education Press, 1971), 34.

3

CHRISTIAN EDUCATION IN HELLENISTIC CITY-STATES

AD 50–400

The second model of disciplined learning that we'll explore shows the new Christian faith meeting the challenge of pluralism. Christianity grew to maturity in a sophisticated urban culture. Adopting the new faith carried a social cost, but leaders emerged to carry forward education, worship, and service amid rival beliefs and practices.

CONTEXT: HELLENISM

Paul and other movement leaders wrote letters to churches in Greek-speaking city-states—Corinth, Philippi, Thessalonica, Colosse, and others. Not even the letter to the Romans is in Latin. All were written in the worldwide language of the time—*koine* (or, common) Greek.

Greek culture was the shared culture of much of the world for centuries. After 323 BC, Alexander the Great's successors founded city-states as outposts of Greek life. Homer, Hesiod, Aristophanes, Plato, Aristotle, and Greek-speaking pathbreakers of drama, philosophy, rhetoric, science, medicine, sculpture, and architecture inspired a cosmopolitan world order. For the first time in history, to be all-a-human-could-be did not depend on membership in one particular race. Human fulfillment hinged on the pursuit of the Greek ideal of humanity. The Greek aspiration for greatness focused on education. Personal honor depended on cultivating oneself. Greece was the civilization of the lifelong learning called *paideia*.[1]

The pursuit of *paideia* meant that social life focused on the learning and religious activities of a gymnasium. Not only a site of athletic competitions, gymnasiums could be found even in larger villages in the Hellenistic world. Sometimes, as when Jerusalem aspired to city-state status, the gymnasium with its naked athletes was a symbol of Hellenization that the conquered, faithful keepers of local culture resisted.[2]

Like globalization in the twenty-first century, Hellenism shifted local cultures toward a fusion. While rural life changed little from centuries past, towns and cities shifted toward Greek-speaking government, Greek arts, Greek sports, and Greek educational institutions. Elites understood that Greek education was the way their children could get ahead in society. Influence spurred Hellenization. In Palestine, for instance, Greek-sympathizing Jewish families did not feel themselves to be denying scriptural faith. The result was a recognizable global culture with distinct local accents.[3]

Rome's takeover of the Mediterranean and Black Sea basins in the century before Christ changed little, culturally or educationally. Greek remained the common language of the empire. Romans pro-

---

[1] H. I. Marrou, *A History of Education in Antiquity*, trans. G. Lamb (Madison and London: University of Wisconsin Press, 1982), 95–101; H. Strathmann, "Polis," *Theological Dictionary of the New Testament*, ed. Gerhard Kittel and Gerhard Friedrich, trans. Geoffrey William Bromiley (Grand Rapids, MI: Eerdmans, 1990); Martin Hengel, *Judaism and Hellenism: Studies in Their Encounter in Palestine During the Early Hellenistic Period*, trans. John Bowden (Philadelphia, PA: Fortress Press, 1981), 64; Michael Azkoul, "The Greek Fathers: Polis and Paideia, Pt II," *St Vladimir's Theological Quarterly* 23, no. 2 (January 1, 1979): 71.

[2] Hengel, *Judaism and Hellenism*, 66–67, 70–75; Cornelia B. Horn and John W. Martens, "*Let the Little Children Come to Me*": *Childhood and Children in Early Christianity* (Washington, DC: CUA Press, 2009), 122; Lester L. Grabbe, "The Hellenistic City of Jerusalem," in *Jews in the Hellenistic and Roman Cities*, ed. John R. Bartlett (London and New York: Routledge, 2002), 6–21.

[3] Grabbe, "The Hellenistic City of Jerusalem," 18.

moted Greek art, literature, architecture, science, and philosophy and accommodated local cultures, as in Judea. The Roman educators Cicero and Varro translated *paideia* as the Latin *humanitas*. This verbal link connects Greek education to Roman education and to our present-day study of the "humanities."[4]

CHRISTIAN LEADERS AND GREEK EDUCATION

Literate education in the empire was an activity for those who had free time, those who didn't need to work to survive, and was therefore pursued by the upper classes. Sons generally followed the father's line of work. Teaching was itself a guild affair. Teachers equipped their sons for what was needed to carry on the family trade. If not used in employment, the ability to write was a luxury. To lose the labor of an able body while paying a tutor would be an investment not possible to many. Besides, a craftsman or a peasant would have little time or ability to instruct a son in reading and writing. Girls' literacy seems to have been accordingly limited, though its extent is debated. "Liberal education" was literally about possessing the liberty and the money to pursue it.[5]

Works by Homer, Hesiod, or Aratus provided the content of literate education—the kind of cultural authorities Paul quotes to the Athenian Areopagus in Acts 17. Learning classical myths, stories, speeches, poems, and plays gave a student the ability to read critically. Studying the language's structure—its grammar—was a means toward the aim of reading and interpreting texts. Only a fraction of students who gained ability to interpret texts went on to higher education with a rhetorician or philosopher.[6]

[4] Hengel, *Judaism and Hellenism*, 64; Michael Azkoul, "The Greek Fathers: Polis and Paideia, Pt I," *St Vladimir's Theological Quarterly* 23, no. 1 (January 1, 1979): 3–21.
[5] Ronald F. Hock, "Paul and Greco-Roman Education," in *Paul in the Greco-Roman World: A Handbook*, ed. J. Paul Sampley (Harrisburg, PA: Trinity Press International, 2003), 204; Joan Petersen, "The Education of Girls in Fourth-Century Rome," in *Christianity and Society: The Social World of Early Christianity*, ed. Everett Ferguson (New York and London: Garland Publishing, 1999), 77–86.
[6] Charles Bigg, *The Church's Task Under the Roman Empire; Four Lectures with Preface, Notes, and an Excursus* (Oxford: Clarendon Press, 1905), 9–20; Emile Durkheim, *The Evolution of Educational Thought: Lectures on the Formation and Development of Secondary Education in France*, trans. P. Collins (London: Routledge & Kegan Paul, 1977), 147–48.

Naturally, the Christian movement outside Palestine relied on Greek literacy. Christians used Greek to access their own Scripture. The Greek Old Testament (or the Septuagint) was the first Christian Bible. The Greek letters and Gospels of Christian movement leaders were eventually compiled as the New Testament. In the first three centuries, Christian leaders were often those with a rhetorical or philosophical education. For example, Paul indicates that he had Greek schooling at Tarsus or Jerusalem (Acts 17, 26; 1 Corinthians 15; Titus 1). Significantly, his arguments are like model writings called *progymnasmata* that were used in the highest Greek education.[7]

STRATEGIC CHRISTIAN EDUCATION

Christians rarely sponsored separate schools in polytheistic city-states. Though Hellenism was wrapped up in a pervasive and attractive education, Christians in the empire did not establish their own schools. Even after Christianity became the empire's official religion in 380, formal schooling in the texts of classical culture continued. Christians established schools for literacy and Latin or Greek that resembled the Hellenistic classical school model only in mission lands outside the empire.[8] Why no separate schools?

The simplest answer is that formal schooling was not considered the place for moral instruction. A variety of sources made up a child's education—tutors for grammar and arithmetic, the gymnasium for physical or musical education, and fathers for their sons' moral formation (Gen. 18:19; Deut. 11:19; Prov. 1:8–9). Parents saw tutors who gave semi-individualized instruction in letters as technicians.

A second reason that Christians rarely developed separate schools was that neither they nor anyone else put much faith in the morality of classicism's texts. Plato famously called down Homer

---

[7] Hock, "Paul and Greco-Roman Education," 204–12; Jerome H. Neyrey, "The Social Location of Paul: Education as the Key," in *Fabrics of Discourse: Essays in Honor of Vernon K. Robbins*, 2003, 126–64; Durkheim, *The Evolution of Educational Thought*, 27–33; Bruce A. Kimball, *Orators and Philosophers: A History of the Idea of Liberal Education* (New York: Teachers College Press, 1986).
[8] Marrou, *A History of Education in Antiquity*, 317.

and the poets for teaching the young that the gods are immoral. Plutarch (c. AD 46–c. 125) instructs teachers to tell pupils that the crazy things poets write are not to be taken seriously. The emperor Julian's persecution in the 300s displaced Christians who were teaching in classical schools. His reason was that they were teaching what they themselves did not believe. A couple of years later, a new emperor restored the Christian teachers. Christians could confidently send their sons to classical schools because they would learn the forms of classical literature and ignore the mythical content. Christian fathers were so sure that the Christian story was true that they had no fear of their young being fooled by what everyone knew was absurd.[9]

Confidence in their alternate history thus empowered Christians to practice family-based countercultural learning. The ancient world's many options for belief—the old gods, the power of the Caesars, Near Eastern cults, multiple philosophies—added up to a massive weariness and fatalism. By contrast, Christ was a sure hope. Israel's God gave truthful words to prophets, to Christ, and to apostles. Jewish history now culminated in Jesus, the Jewish Messiah. Scripture told a universal narrative. "Jesus is Lord" was at least as universal a claim as the empire's "Caesar is Lord." The Christians proclaimed the authoritative account of world history and its anticipated end. Scripture's spare style, unlike the elaborations of Homer, underscored that it set out to depict reality. Besides its narrative sections, its poetry, laws, prophecy, worship songs, proverbs, and apocalyptic writings all applied the narrative. Thus, a distinctive confidence flowed from the confession that Israel's Savior was Lord.[10]

---

[9] Marrou, *A History of Education in Antiquity*, 314–29; Benjamin D. Wayman, "Julian against Christian Educators: Julian and Basil on a Proper Education," *Christian Scholar's Review* 45, no. 3 (Spring 2016): 249–67; David L. Balch, "Paul, Families, and Households," in *Paul in the Greco-Roman World: A Handbook*, ed. J. Paul Sampley, vol. 1 (Harrisburg, PA: Trinity Press International, 2003), 198–227.

[10] David Bentley Hart, *Atheist Delusions: The Christian Revolution and Its Fashionable Enemies* (New Haven, CT: Yale University Press, 2009), 131–45; Charles Norris Cochrane, *Christianity and Classical Culture: A Study of Thought and Action from Augustus to Augustine* (Oxford: Oxford University Press, 1957), 156–76; Erich Auerbach, *Mimesis: The Representation of Reality in Western Literature*, trans. Willard R. Trask, vol. 548 (Princeton, NJ: Princeton University

Prospective church members—*catechumens*—learned a universal history, the destiny of the world, and the meaning of their lives. The earliest creed asserted salvation history as fact, organized in three sections by each person of the Trinity. Reciters confessed, "I believe in Jesus Christ (who) suffered under Pontius Pilate, was crucified, died, and was buried." The words of the creed seem to draw most from Luke's Gospel. The object of faith is God—Father, Son, and Spirit. "I believe in God . . ." is the headline. The cornerstone of the new faith was confidence in the resurrection of the Savior of Israel. The creed does not confess Scripture itself as an article of faith, but its affirmations outline Israel's Scripture and the apostolic writings. Leaving behind Israel's God-given seventh day (Saturday), the early churches moved their day of worship to the day when Christ was raised, the first of the week (Sunday). The move indicates their great confidence. A new day of God's dealings with humanity had dawned.[11]

The movement took initiation seriously. In the first centuries, the best-known church leaders made a high priority of teaching new believers. In the second century, Bishops Irenaeus and Tertullian wrote catecheses that expounded the stages of salvation history. The fullest surviving catechesis is from Cyril of Jerusalem in the fourth century. His lectures are on oral preparation, penitence, God's mercy, baptism, summary of the dogma, confirmation, the Eucharist, and lines of the Apostles' Creed. It is fitting that the city of Alexandria's catechetical school was also Christianity's first higher education.[12]

The missionary statesman Lesslie Newbigin (1909–1998) underlined how much Christians in the present-day West need to

Press, 1953); James Barr, *The Concept of Biblical Theology: An Old Testament Perspective* (Minneapolis: Fortress Press, 2009).

[11] Kirsopp Lake, "The Apostles' Creed," *Harvard Theological Review* 17, no. 2 (1924): 173–183.

[12] Clinton E. Arnold, "Early Church Catechesis and New Christians' Classes in Contemporary Evangelicalism," *Journal of the Evangelical Theological Society* 47, no. 1 (2004): 45; Annewies van den Hoek, "The 'Catechetical' School of Early Christian Alexandria and Its Philonic Heritage," *Harvard Theological Review* 90, no. 1 (January 1997): 59–87; George T. Kurian, "Catechesis in the Early Church," ed. George T. Kurian and Mark A. Lamport, *Encyclopedia of Christian Education* (Lanham, MD: Rowman & Littlefield Publishers, 2015).

recover that early confidence in their story. They need to recover Scripture as a single story. John Cassian (c. 360–435) achieved the unified witness of the Bible from Abraham to the apostles by his distinctive approach to interpretation. He developed a multilevel reading strategy to square difficult passages of the Old Testament with the New Testament. Using Cassian's method, readers looked for a literal sense first, then a spiritual sense that included allegorical, moral, and future aspects. Cassian's allegorizing method could draw meanings from Scripture without much restraint. Western Christians may not want to recycle his reading strategy entirely, but they do need to recapture his ability to read the book as a unified story. Only renewed confidence can empower renewed education.[13]

PHILOSOPHICAL SPOILS

Christian leaders in the first centuries taught that Greek philosophy was vain, subtle, contradictory, artificial—and superseded by the truth of the Gospels. As the "foreign" philosophy, Greek philosophy was the ultimate hazard because it was the ultimate defense of the classical worldview and its city-state. Paul had already contrasted the wisdom of the world that crucified Christ with God's wisdom (1 Corinthians 1–4).[14]

The North African Christian leader Tertullian (c. 155–c. 240) articulated a hands-off position. He denied any connection between "Jerusalem" and "Athens"—between revealed knowledge and philosophic speculations. For Tertullian, Scripture contained all that one needed to know. On the other hand, some Christians found the style and content of classical writings deeply attractive. Jerome (347–420) once dreamed that Christ the judge rebuked him for being no Christian but a "Ciceronian." He said Jerome loved classical learning more than him. Jerome woke up in shock. Ultimately, Augustine's

---

[13] N. T. Wright, "How Can the Bible Be Authoritative?," *Vox Evangelica* 21, no. 1991 (1991): 7–32; Michael W. Goheen, "The Urgency of Reading the Bible as One Story," *Theology Today* 64, no. 4 (January 2008): 469–83.
[14] Azkoul, "The Greek Fathers, pt I," 5.

approach to philosophy, a century after Tertullian, found the middle way. Augustine (354–430) urged that believers should discern what is false in classical thinking, but in effect take prizes of war from it. They should accept the "gold" that conforms to Christian beliefs, just as the Israelites took gold from the Egyptians when departing for the Promised Land.[15]

Augustine thought deeply about words and teaching. He recognized that human words could tell about God's triune reality only in limited ways. Human finiteness in time and space, plus effects from the fall, make human speech only approximate. In complete contrast to modern rationalists and empiricists, Augustine says that our words are less and less reliable about ultimate reality as they are clearer and more definite. Instead, one must depend on Scripture as a lifeline to truth. One must seek to read it as accurately as possible. Revelation gives heavenly realities in earthly words—however liable to human misunderstanding the words are.[16]

As Christian conceptions met classical objectors, Greek philosophy began to show value. Philosophy gave Christian leaders categories and a vocabulary to answer doubters with apologetics and theology. Church councils defined and elaborated beliefs in philosophical language, yielding an orthodox way to understand the one God of Israel as subsisting in three persons. The classical scholar Charles Cochrane emphasizes that Christianity's victory in the Roman Empire represented an intellectual victory over the classical worldview, one that came after three centuries of deep engagement.[17]

FRAMEWORKS OF PAIDEIA

For Paul, teaching is not for forming an able intellect or simply gathering formal knowledge. The New Testament Gospels and letters show only occasional interest in formal schooling. Paul uses

---

[15] David K. Naugle, *Worldview: The History of a Concept* (Grand Rapids, MI: Eerdmans, 2002), 259.
[16] C. Ando, "Augustine on Language," *Revue d'Etudes Augustiniennes et Patristiques* 40, no. 1 (January 1, 1994): 45–78; Edward Morgan, *The Incarnation of the Word: The Theology of Language of Augustine of Hippo* (London and New York: T & T Clark, 2010), 39.
[17] Cochrane, *Christianity and Classical Culture*.

the categories of Hellenism in 1 Corinthians 1–4 to show how God ended human pretentions to superior wisdom. Where knowledge puffs one up (1 Cor. 8:1), Christ the apparent foolishness of God is God's true wisdom (1 Cor. 1:22–24). The Hellenistic concern for ongoing cultivation was dramatically deepened by Jesus's personalized covenant radicalism, as in the Sermon on the Mount. Paul explains a historically grounded paideia that his culture could understand but one concerned less with head knowledge than with heart knowledge. Paideia went on steroids.[18]

Paul's Christian paideia aims for dynamic community transformation toward the image of Christ. The New Testament letters see church life as witness to a truly better way. Jesus is the new Adam. The urgent concern of the epistles was to encourage the community to live Christian beliefs. Paul teaches churches the principles that inform his responses to specific situations. Unlike the contemporary difference between preaching and teaching, the New Testament makes little distinction between the two. Education in the widest sense—cultural storytelling—is what the earliest churches existed to do. Accordingly, education in the widest sense—Memory, Vision, Symbols, and Ethos—consumed their attention.[19]

Paul works out his Christian paideia by two metaphors: the *oikos*, the extended household of God, and the *ekklesia*, the gathering of an alternative city-state.

OIKOS

The *oikos* metaphor drives many New Testament descriptions. Households in the Greco-Roman world included a nuclear family of husband, wife, and children, plus relatives including the elderly, plus slaves and other servants, plus sons adopted into the household. Archaeology

---

[18] Diana Swancutt, "Scripture 'Reading' and Identity Formation in Paul: Paideia among Believing Greeks" (Society of Biblical Literature, Paul and Scripture Seminar, Washington, DC, 2006).

[19] J. Stanley Glen, *The Recovery of the Teaching Ministry* (Philadelphia, PA: Westminster Press, 1960); Robert C. Worley, *Preaching and Teaching in the Earliest Church* (Philadelphia, PA: Westminster Press, 1967).

indicates that households were open places for gatherings; the more invited or uninvited people who were around it, the more influential the household. Thus in 1 Corinthians 14, Paul assumes that unbelievers might appear in the course of worship. Christians formed a household of God that contrasted with neighboring households.

"Edifying" is thus the educative process for an *oikos*. Paul's metaphor imagines leaders as builders who are edifying or building up (Eph. 2:21). When Paul speaks of teaching house to house in Acts 20:20, he means house-church by house-church. Dedicated buildings for worship services did not appear for decades. Christianity grew as a network of house churches in a city. Among these units, an *oikos* or household of God was to be built up, just as a temple for true worship was constructed stone by stone. The household of God has only one foundation—Christ (Romans 1 and 16). Building up a household is an appropriately flexible metaphor for educating God's family.[20]

The *oikos* metaphor allowed Christians to use and redefine cultural practices. Husbands, wives, children, and slaves of the household needed to learn a household code of conduct (Eph. 5:21–6:9; Col. 3:18–4:1; 1 Pet. 3:1–6). In the household of God, older generations were to model Christian teaching to the young. Slavish copying was not the intention. Teachers such as Paul were models that less mature Christians could follow, and in turn, inculcate the original (Christ) into themselves. Settled pastors appear to have been rare. After the apostolic era, visiting prophets and teachers continued to make circuits of the cities, as they do with rapidly growing African churches of the present day. With no formal preparation, they gleaned what they could (1 John 4:1). Learning the faith in a household was done in a context where the knowledge was immediately applied.[21]

---

[20] James Francis, "Household," ed. David Noel Freedman, *Eerdmans Dictionary of the Bible* (Grand Rapids, MI: Eerdmans, 2000), 613–14.

[21] Balch, "Paul, Families, and Households"; Philip E. Morrison, "Implications of Paul's Model for Leadership Training in Light of Church Growth in Africa," *Africa Journal of Evangelical Theology* 30 (2011): 56; Valeriy A. Alikin, *The Earliest History of the Christian Gathering: Origin, Development and Content of the Christian Gathering in the First to Third Centuries*, vol.102, Supplements to

Recent anthropology investigates "situated learning." When a West African tailor learns his craft, he learns it in a tailor's shop under experienced tailors. Learning is by observation and imitation as well as by direct instruction and coaching. The learning is "situated" where it will be applied. If the context of learning does not demand and encourage application, the knowledge will be forgotten. The learning is all relevant to the learner. It is not abstract or of potential application in the future.[22]

Unsituated learning is a significant issue for present-day, church-related learning. The weakening of contexts where biblical knowledge matters may help explain declines in Bible reading and Bible knowledge. Families that practice the faith and teach it in the home remain the primary site of faith learning. Renewed Christian education must show the urgent cultural relevance of God's Word.

EKKLESIA

Ekklesia is Paul's second metaphor of Christian living for his alternate paideia. This metaphor requires some unpacking in order to be understood. *Ekklesia* is a noun for assemblies when a city-state came together to enact a drama or determine political action. The English term *church* translates the New Testament Greek word *ekklesia*.

Shared religious activities were the glue of city-states. Drama's origin was a collective working of humans under the gods. The civic *ekklesia* enacted a scenario in which actors and audience joined together. Held in honor of a city's god, civic religious

Vigiliae Christianae (Leiden and Boston: Brill, 2010), 207; Glen Thompson, "Teaching the Teachers: Pastoral Education in the Early Church," *Wisconsin Lutheran Quarterly* 94, no. 2 (1997): 103–14; Jo-Ann A. Brant, "The Place of Mimēsis in Paul's Thought," *Studies in Religion/Sciences Religieuses* 22, no. 3 (1993): 285–300.

[22] Jean Lave, "A Comparative Approach to Educational Forms and Learning Processes," *Anthropology & Education Quarterly* 13, no. 2 (1982): 181–87; Lave, "Situating Learning in Communities of Practice," in *Perspectives on Socially Shared Cognition*, vol. 2, 1991, 63–82; Jean Lave and Etienne Wenger, *Situated Learning: Legitimate Peripheral Participation* (Cambridge and New York: Cambridge University Press, 1991); Iona Hine, "The Quest for Biblical Literacy: Curricula, Culture, and Case Studies," in *Rethinking Biblical Literacy*, ed. Katie B. Edwards (London: Bloomsbury, 2015), 47–67; Charles R. Foster, *From Generation to Generation: The Adaptive Challenge of Mainline Protestant Education in Forming Faith* (Eugene, OR: Cascade Books, 2012), 96–119.

festivals could feature drama as well as sacrifices, epic song competitions, and athletic competitions. Loyalty to the city-state was
summed up by loyalty to its gods. Good citizens sought to give all
gods their due, especially their most important gods. Acts 19 tells
of the riot that broke out when silversmiths whose livelihoods came
from religion incited the crowd to chant "Great is Diana of the
Ephesians" against the Christian missionaries.[23]

Ekklesia as an alternative city-state appears in the New
Testament at Ephesians 2:12–19, Philippians 3:20, and 1 Peter
2:11. Early Christians contrasted the Hellenistic *polis* to their
heavenly community. The Christian king is in heaven. In the
Greek translation of the Old Testament, the Septuagint, *ekklesia* appears when Israel gathers as a body. In the New Testament
letters, God's special people embody an alternative heavenly
polis—spiritual Jerusalem—in Galatians 4:25–26, Hebrews 11
and 12, and Revelation 11 and 21. Christians never seem to have
called their own gatherings "synagogues," though the Jewish
synagogue provided a partial model. Clement of Rome's first
letter speaks of a polis of God in the early second century, and
the Alexandrian Christian leaders Clement and Origen rely on
the idea of a Christian polis in the third century.[24] At the end
of the fourth century, John Chrysostom informs baptism candidates that the purpose of their "training" is to prepare them for
"citizenship." "For we have been enrolled as citizens of another
state, the heavenly Jerusalem."[25]

---

[23] Strathmann, "Polis"; Robert Parker, "Greek Religion," in *The Oxford History of the Classical World*, ed. John Boardman, Jasper Griffin, and Oswyn Murray (Oxford: Oxford University Press, 1986), 272; Oddone Longo, "Theatre of the Polis," in *Nothing to Do with Dionysos?: Athenian Drama in Its Social Context*, ed. John J. Winkler and Froma I. Zeitlin (Princeton, NJ: Princeton University Press, 1992); Stephanie van Willigenburg and C. Marshall, "Judging Athenian Dramatic Competitions," *Journal of Hellenic Studies* 124 (2004): 90–107; Philip A. Harland, "The Declining Polis? Religious Rivalries in Ancient Civic Context," in *Religious Rivalries in the Early Roman Empire and the Rise of Christianity*, ed. Leif E. Vaage, Studies in Christianity and Judaism 18 (Waterloo, Ontario: Wilfrid Laurier University Press, 2006), 21–49.

[24] Clement of Rome's first letter (Ch. 64); see J. B. Lightfoot, ed., *The Apostolic Fathers*, Part 1, S. Clement of Rome, vol. 1 (London: Macmillan, 1890), accessed August 28, 2018, http://archive.org /details/p1apostolicfathe01clemuoft.

[25] Bapt. Instr. Ill, 5; IV, 29, quoted in Azkoul, "The Greek Fathers, pt II," January 1, 1979, 67, 72.

Christian *ekklesia* thus were an alternative civic gathering in contrast to the dominant culture. For believers, worship was the drama that recapitulated the most important events of human history. Easter and Christmas made twin foci for the year's rhythm. Christians reenacted the sacred story by a calendar of rituals. They regularly shared the Savior's body and blood as bread and wine and so shared his very life. Rituals translated the dying and rising Son of God into a shared covenant meal allowing believers to participate in the death and resurrection of Christ. In baptism, penitents were immersed and raised again from water. While the ceremony over time altered the amount of water and the possible subjects of the ritual, the meaning remained the same: participation in the death and resurrection of the Son of God. Worship rituals brought initiates into the realism of Christian history.[26]

Rituals together retold the story into which an initiate was inducted. Mysteries were a religious phenomenon in the ancient world. In mysteries such as those of the Greek Eleusis, the Persian Mithras, or the Egyptian Osiris, participants gained secret knowledge after an initiation ritual, though the beliefs were not codified as systems. An initiate had an extraordinary experience about which he was forbidden to speak afterward. The term translated as "mystery" appears at numerous places in Paul's letters, prominently in Ephesians (3:3–6, 9–10; 5:31–32).

The initiation process casts light into a mystery/initiation on the Christian process. During their initiation period, catechumens were dismissed from the most meaning-laden portions of a service—they were not ready to hear and participate. Joining the *ekklesia* was not a casual commitment. The early church leader Hippolytus refers to catechumens being taught three years under

---

[26] Susan Elliott, "Mystery Cults," ed. David Noel Freedman and Allen C. Myers, *Eerdmans Dictionary of the Bible* (Grand Rapids, MI: Eerdmans, 2000), 931–32; Donn F. Morgan, "Education," ed. David Noel Freedman, Astrid B. Beck, and Allen C. Myers, *Eerdmans Dictionary of the Bible* (Grand Rapids, MI: Eerdmans, 2000); Harland, "The Declining Polis?"; Stanley Samuel Harakas, "Faith Formation in Byzantium," in *Educating People of Faith: Exploring the History of Jewish and Christian Communities*, ed. John H. Van Engen (Grand Rapids, MI: Eerdmans, 2004), 127–29.

the care of an elder. Candidates came to instruction with a sponsor, not unlike the companion slave who brought students to a tutor.[27]

Yet for Paul, the Christian mystery had become public knowledge—he connected it with Christ's public crucifixion (1 Cor. 1:23; 2:1–7). Missional theologian Lesslie Newbigin calls Christian revelation an "open secret." Where the mysteries lacked codified beliefs, the church wanted its rituals to be understood. Church practices and beliefs were fused. In later centuries, "mystagogical" sermons explained church rituals to those who would participate.[28]

The early churches reinforced bare catechetical knowledge by "situating" the knowledge where it was to be used. Today, writers call for recovery of whole-person learning in church contexts, including renewed patterns of ritual. Early churches expressed the faith by a ritual system that embodied Christian beliefs. Bodily action enacted the revealed mystery of Christ, in communion, baptism, and catechumenate.

An effect of media-saturated societies is that all personal action is overwhelmingly "mediated," not immediate and not "real." Even family life appears at one remove, as social media snapshots or clips. Rituals reflecting spiritual realities could restore a lost dimension in Western social life. Restoring a ritual counterpart to beliefs can situate the learning so it matters and is better remembered.[29]

SUMMARY OF CHRISTIAN EDUCATION IN HELLENISTIC CITY-STATES

Curriculum, as previously discussed, is a threefold, embodied, meaning-making system. It includes a stated, formal curriculum

---

[27] Edwin Hatch, *The Influence of Greek Ideas on Christianity* (London: Williams and Norgate, 1891); Marrou, *A History of Education in Antiquity*, 315.
[28] Walter Burkert, *Ancient Mystery Cults* (Cambridge: Harvard University Press, 1987), 66–87; William Harmless, *Augustine and the Catechumenate* (Collegeville, MN: Liturgical Press, 1995), 69; Christopher Dawson, *Education and the Crisis of Christian Culture* (Chicago: Regnery, 1949), 9; Enrico Mazza, *Mystagogy: A Theology of Liturgy in the Patristic Age* (Liturgical Press, 1989), ix–x.
[29] Thomas De Zengotita, "The Numbing of the American Mind: Culture as Anesthetic," *Harpers Magazine*, April 2002; Thomas De Zengotita, *Mediated: How the Media Shapes Our World and the Way We Live in It* (New York: Bloomsbury Publishing USA, 2006); Zygmunt Bauman, *Liquid Modernity* (Cambridge, UK, and Malden, MA: Polity Press, 2000), 118–29; Zygmunt Bauman, *Liquid Times: Living in an Age of Uncertainty* (John Wiley & Sons, 2013).

worked through in a hidden or structural curriculum that ignores a null curriculum. The curriculum takes selected knowledge to initiate learners into the Memory, Vision, Symbols and Ethos of a culture or subculture.

Christians in the Greco-Roman era continued Jesus's practice of reconfiguring majority culture for their own purposes, including processes of education. They sharply disagreed with their mainstream society about power, money, and sex. However, they used some forms of the culture such as household structures, educational practices, and ritual patterns for their own purposes, turning them inside out.

- Their **Memory** was the tradition of Jesus, crucified as a criminal, risen alive, ascended as Lord of the cosmos and Lord of the decaying Roman society as of all societies.
- Their **Vision** was a transformed universe ruled by a gracious God, already present in the reign of the Messiah.
- Their **Symbols** asserted and ritually enacted the story of Jesus.
- Their practices attracted contempt and ridicule, but the sacrificial **Ethos** of care for neighbors, sexual renunciation, as well as their willingness to die in witness for Christ, finally commanded respect in a power-oriented but worn-out society.

The stated curriculum for Christians was a catechesis of scriptural history and creeds. Households underwrote learning by making worship central in their homes. The hidden or structural processes were the ritual pathway of initiation into the church body. Rituals expanded their learning by enacting it. The null curriculum, naturally, was that which was disbelieved and discounted, such as Greek myth and unreconstructed philosophy.

Christian education in Hellenism shows that educators must reclaim certainty as key to the faith. Only an education certain about its content will persist. Hellenistic Christianity's perseverance came from its certainty about God. Because Christianity arises from revelation, renewal comes when believers return to its source. The earliest Christian experience indicates that taking Scripture seriously will accompany renewed education. The physical world speaks of God adequately; Scripture enables believers to read the book of nature rightly, as the sixteenth-century Protestant Reformer John Calvin noted. By faith, believers understand that God created the world from nothing (Hebrews 11). Mediated reality makes it hard to appreciate the significance of God's creation of the world.[30]

The capacity to tell a persuasive countercultural story made Christian education successful in the Greco-Roman world. The Christian subculture in North America finds itself in a severe competition of stories. Youth exposure to mass media, now full-time by handheld devices, eclipses exposure to the Christian story. Moreover, the withering of settings for acting out the Christian story means that Christian knowledge is increasingly "unsituated." It lacks a relevant setting for its use.

The earliest churches prevailed over their severe competition. Their deliberate alienation from the wider culture placed significant weight on family and church formation in faith. Contradictory voices and stories were kept away. Christians maintained the faith in high tension with their society. In some places and periods, the sacrifice of lives was graphic illustration of their nonconformity. Their education made them ready to place their lives on the line.

---

[30] John Calvin, *Institutes of the Christian Religion*, ed. John T. McNeill, trans. Ford Lewis Battles, vol. XX and XXI, Library of Christian Classics (Philadelphia, PA: Westminster Press, 1960), I:VI:1.

4

CLOISTERED EDUCATION

500–1200

An essay by Herbert Spencer poses an educational master question: "What knowledge is of most worth?" In forty-four pages, Spencer—Victorian England's popular philosopher—gave his answer.

Imagine human needs from basic to advanced. The most basic need, before all others, is knowledge for self-preservation. After survival comes knowledge for nurturing the next generation. Next is knowledge of social and political life. At the narrow top, Spencer places leisure activities and other personal preferences, including religious knowledge.[1]

Spencer's plan of "knowledge of most worth" is for purposeful living within present-day societies.[2] The knowledge of most worth can be empirically validated in this present world. His pyramid of needs—survival, procreation, social life, and "leisure"—foreshadows the hierarchies of cognitive, behavioral, and affective outcomes that shape modern public-school curricula.[3]

---

[1] Herbert Spencer, "What Knowledge Is of Most Worth?," in *Education: Intellectual, Moral, and Physical* (New York: Hurst and Company, 1862), 5–92.

[2] George R. Knight, "What Knowledge Is of Most Worth? Adventist Colleges and the Search for Meaning," *Journal of Adventist Education* 54 (1991): 5–8; Spencer, "What Knowledge Is of Most Worth?," 18.

[3] Benjamin S. Bloom, ed., *Taxonomy of Educational Objectives: The Classification of Educational Goals, Handbook I: Cognitive Domain* (New York and London: Longman's, Green and Co., 1956); David R. Krathwohl, Benjamin S. Bloom, and Bertram B. Masia, *Taxonomy of Educational Objectives: The Classification of Educational Goals, Handbook II: Affective Domain* (New York and London: Longman Group Ltd., 1964); David R. Krathwohl, "A Revision of Bloom's Taxonomy: An Overview," *Theory into Practice* 41, no. 4 (2002): 212–18.

Spencer asked an important question—even if one does not accept his answer. All educations impart "knowledge of most worth."

Nearly no European in the years 500 to 1200 would have answered as Spencer. What knowledge was most important to medieval Christians? And, how did the pursuit of Christian knowledge lead to the Christian schools and universities that developed across Europe during that time?[4]

An answer to the formative Christian era's "worthy knowledge" question is not just of museum interest. Western educational practices begun in the Middle Ages include academic gowns, convocation, commencements, diplomas, professors, and thesis defenses. These Symbols and rituals continue to have meaning today. They are deep cultural habits formed in the era we'll call "cloistered education."

FROM THE GROUND UP

When Roman administration withdrew from Europe, safe urban economic hubs and local church life withered all over Europe. In England, for example, Rome's effective withdrawal came in the early 400s.[5]

In the years that followed, unchristianized peoples migrated into lands no longer defended. Not long after this shift, men who had taken vows to dedicate themselves to God (monks and friars) arrived on mission. For example, the Irish monk Columbanus and companions arrived in Burgundy, eastern France, around AD 585. They evangelized that area, and young converts began to gather with them. The result was a single-sex Christian community where monks prayed, studied, cultivated fields, and evangelized. Columbanus's

---

[4] Emile Durkheim makes this point strongly in *The Evolution of Educational Thought: Lectures on the Formation and Development of Secondary Education in France*, trans. P. Collins (London: Routledge & Kegan Paul, 1977), 3–14.

[5] Peter Ackroyd, *Foundation: The History of England from Its Earliest Beginnings to the Tudors* (New York: Thomas Dunne, 2011), 38–39; Peter John Heather, *Empires and Barbarians: Migration, Development and the Birth of Europe* (London: Macmillan, 2009); Peter Brown, *The Rise of Western Christendom: Triumph and Diversity, A.D. 200–1000* (Chichester, UK and Malden, MA: Wiley-Blackwell, 2013).

monastery at Luxeuil sent out at least sixty-three missionaries, resulting in a hundred more monasteries. Irish monks brought Celtic Christianity to Belgium, Switzerland, Austria, southern Germany, and northern Italy. Monks and clergy set up monasteries and cathedral communities as hubs of mission activity. Another example: in 597, the Roman church sent a missionary and colleagues to convert England to the Catholic faith. Named after the earlier bishop of Hippo, this second Augustine set up his cathedral community at Canterbury in the southeastern countryside. There, he commenced a mission to the king of Kent and neighboring kingdoms.[6]

Both monasteries and cathedral cloisters were enclosed ascetic communities under a spiritual leader and separated from the surrounding secular society. A cathedral community accepted the leadership of its bishop. In cathedrals and monasteries, a candidate gained membership after a trial period by taking extraordinary vows not sought from all baptized members of the church. Monasteries, led by an abbot, conformed to a severe daily rhythm of fasting, praying, working, and reading. Benedict's rule, the constitution of most monasteries, also allowed study time in a monk's routine.[7]

To continue its life into the future, a monastery accepted *oblates*—pre-teen males, sometimes older—whose parents offered them for monastic life. At cathedrals, parents brought sons to train as future priests. The need to teach for the future meant that some older members would become teachers. At a cathedral, the bishop or his officers taught. Schools were not always continuous, but while novices were learning their letters, both cathedrals and monasteries taught. For example, in 796, Charlemagne's court educator Alcuin urged Eanbald II, archbishop

---

[6] Durkheim, *The Evolution of Educational Thought*, 30; Jean Décarreaux, *Monks and Civilization: From the Barbarian Invasions to the Reign of Charlemagne*, trans. Charlotte Haldane (London: Allen & Unwin, 1964), 192; Daryll McCarthy, "Hearts and Minds Aflame for Christ: Irish Monks—a Model for Academic Missions," *Christian Scholarship . . . for What?* (Grand Rapids, MI: 2001); Robin Mackintosh, *Augustine of Canterbury: Leadership, Spirituality and Mission* (Norwich, UK: Canterbury Press, 2013); Henry Mayr-Harting, *Coming of Christianity to Anglo-Saxon England* (University Park, PA: Penn State Press, 2010), 69–70.

[7] Margaret Deanesly, *A History of the Medieval Church, 590–1500* (London: Methuen, 1925), 87.

of York that "Your grace [should] provide teachers for the boys. There should be classes for reading, singing, and writing separate from the clergy, and separate teachers for each class."[8]

True worship in the Catholic tradition required Latin. Novices in cathedrals or monasteries needed to learn the language for worship, so they could understand Scripture and the creed. Learning Latin meant mastering morphology and syntax, translating from English to Latin, writing Latin prose and verse, possibly speaking the language. Choir boys needed to learn to read Latin well enough to sing—even if they sang without understanding it. For example, when Psalm 22 came up in the church cycle, boys would be required to chant, "*Deus Deus meus respice me quare me dereliquisti*" ("My God, my God, look upon me, why hast thou forsaken me?"). Language and literature to understand the Bible and, later, to understand classical literature, were thus central subjects for both choristers and grammarians. The crucial fact is that all subjects revolved around the church. Any mathematic teaching was simply exercises on how to compute the date of Easter—a longstanding controversy important in church life.[9]

Cloisters, learning, and training of the next generation were bound together. Christian mission and Christian education went ahead together. Augustine of Canterbury tackled his mission with the Latin prayer book in one hand and the Latin grammar book in the other. Schooling developed under church control; no one could open a school in a bishop's diocese without a license, under

---

[8] Jo Ann Hoeppner Moran, *The Growth of English Schooling, 1340–1548: Learning, Literacy, and Laicization in Pre-Reformation York Diocese*, Princeton Legacy Library (Princeton, NJ: Princeton University Press, 2014), 21–22; Nicholas Orme, *Medieval Schools: From Roman Britain to Renaissance England* (New Haven, CT: Yale University Press, 2006), 18; J. W. Adamson, "Education," in *The Legacy of the Middle Ages*, ed. C. G. Crump and E. F. Jacob (Oxford: Clarendon Press, 1926), 256.

[9] Nicholas Orme, "For Richer, For Poorer?: Free Education in England, c.1380–1530," *The Journal of the History of Childhood and Youth* 1, no. 2 (May 25, 2008): 172; Adamson, "Education," 255; Raymond Williams, *The Long Revolution* (London: Chatto & Windus, 1961), 5, 7; H. I. Marrou, *A History of Education in Antiquity*, trans. G. Lamb (Madison and London: University of Wisconsin Press, 1982), 325.

penalty of trial in a church court. Thus the first formal European education was no more and no less than an arm of the church.[10]

Three aspects of the earliest Western Christian education help explain present-day education: (1) the intensive nature of schooling, (2) a sacred-secular split, and (3) the priority of general ideas.

INTENSIVE SCHOOLING

Why did men or women imagine that living in a single-sex enclosed community would make their personal salvation more likely? The growing wealth of established churches starting in Egypt and moving west, led some Christians to withdraw. The first monasticism seems to have filled a space left empty when persecutions faded. No longer could one give a supreme witness to Christ by giving one's life.

A central Bible passage that urged withdrawers toward monasticism was Jesus's advice to the rich young ruler: "If you would be perfect, go, sell what you possess and give to the poor, and you will have treasure in heaven; and come, follow me" (Matt. 19:21). While present-day readers tend to read the advice as given to one who loved wealth too much, early Christians read it as advised to all. The New Testament has strands of ethical idealism. Sometimes it reads as if virtue should be added to virtue. Peter urges believers to "make every effort to supplement your faith with virtue, and virtues with knowledge," and so on (2 Pet. 1:5–15). Clement's epistle in the early second century emphasizes virtue development even more. Writing to the church at Corinth, Clement does not urge them to love one another as Paul had done earlier in 1 Corinthians 13; instead, he urges a Stoic-style inner discipline for believers. He imagines the church as an army brigade advancing the kingdom of God. The Didache's author, also in the second century, contrasts two ways—the way of life and the way of death—but its prescriptions are ethical

---

ones. Virtue development lines up with the whole Greek tradition. Christian faith moved toward the Greek understanding of life as personal development or paideia. In this context, Jesus's words, "If you would be perfect," seemed to tell Christians to assure their salvation by a dedicated ascetic life.[11]

Every Christian took vows at his or her baptism; the first monks saw themselves as only living out the vows. "Early Monasticism was not an ecclesiastical institution. It was precisely a spontaneous movement, a drive. And it was distinctively a lay movement." Radical Christians reacted against lukewarm faith. To be saved, they believed one must strive for perfect holiness.[12]

Monastery and cloister schools taught this desire management. A monastery or a bishop's cloister walled off temptations that came in regular life. Important among those temptations were bodily desires. Already in Paul's first letter to the Corinthian Christians, married life is a concession to weak members who lack the gift of celibacy. As personal virtue became the surest sign of salvation this side of Judgment Day, bodily desires more and more appeared as a hazard. Future clergy and monks sought salvation by keeping desires under control. The pursuit of salvation through self-control bred stern inner discipline.[13]

Desire management brought perspectives on thought life too. Intellectual desires could be as out of joint as bodily desires. Take "curiosity" for example: modern-era people consider curiosity a good thing, but medieval people, following Augustine of Hippo, saw curiosity as possibly good and possibly bad. They recognized that one could seek knowledge from *amor sciendi*, as a "studious"

[11] David Bentley Hart, "Christ's Rabble," *Commonweal Magazine*, accessed December 16, 2016, https://www.commonwealmagazine.org/christs-rabble; Samuel Gregg, "Christians, Capitalism, and Culture: A Response to David Bentley Hart," *Public Discourse* (blog), accessed December 11, 2015, http://www.thepublicdiscourse.com/2015/12/16117/; Werner Jaeger, *Early Christianity and Greek Paideia* (Cambridge, UK: Belknap Press, 1961), 16–26.
[12] Georges Florovsky, "Empire and Desert: Antinomies of Christian History," *The Greek Orthodox Theological Review* 3, no. 2 (1957): 146–48.
[13] Peter R. L. Brown, *The Body and Society: Men, Women, and Sexual Renunciation in Early Christianity* (New York: Columbia University Press, 1988), 7–64.

person. Alternately, the desire to know can come from the disordered desire of *curiositas*. Chasing after an ambulance or peeking in a window is probably not seeking knowledge from genuine love. Augustine thought curiosity could be a kind of lust. The desire to know may be good or bad, depending on what a person ultimately loves and seeks. Only genuine love wants to know for good reasons.

Cloistered schooling was a revolution without precedent. For the first time, a school brought all subjects into a single point of view. By contrast, classical schooling shopped around for tutors with a variety of points of view. Springing from a faith in which right beliefs and attitudes are supremely important, cloistered schooling became a comprehensive environment. Intense moral training was a new thing. Cloistered education realized that what might be achieved in an instant—full conversion, or, salvation—could be achieved also by slow, steady pressure in a special environment. It is deeply significant that education in the West arose from a movement deeply concerned about external and internal holiness. Though the beliefs it strives to foster have changed over time, schooling in the West retained the concern for deep personal formation.[14]

Beliefs naturally affected practices. Pursuit of knowledge as good or bad led to discipline. In modern-era schooling, bored pupils indicate bad teaching. Such an assessment is because modern-era people see children as basically good. For cloistered teachers—almost all Augustinians—children and adults were born sinners. Boredom was a moral problem to do with pupils, not with the teacher. Where was the pupil in his formation toward perfection? If he was bored, perhaps his mind was where it should not be. Bodily punishment for intellectual sins seemed logical.[15]

---

[14] Durkheim, *The Evolution of Educational Thought*, 27–33; Marrou, *A History of Education in Antiquity*, 319.

[15] Catherine Chin, "Telling Boring Stories: Time, Narrative, and Pedagogy in De Catechizandis Rudibus," *Augustinian Studies* 37, no. 1 (January 2006): 61; Paul J. Griffiths, "The Vice of Curiosity," *Pro Ecclesia* 15, no. 1 (2006): 47–63.

FROM NARRATIVE TO PROPOSITIONS

The second continuing attribute of cloistered education was its abstract quality.

Why is the sound and feel of the Sermon on Mount so different from the sound and feel of the Nicene Creed? The question was asked by the historian of ideas, Edwin Hatch, a century ago. How did Jesus's words with their prophetic personal impact become a set of propositions? True Christian knowledge is not only a form of words.[16]

One reason for the reduction of personal knowledge to verbal knowledge is that centuries of engagement with Greco-Roman philosophy moved the Christian faith to a philosophical expression. Philosophy taught Christian leaders to write clear statements of belief. Philosophy, in a sense, became theology's "handmaid." Philosophical or abstracted knowledge is true outside of history and time. Philosophy tended to shift faith away from reliance on an event in history toward a systematic confession. Christ's life, death, resurrection, and ascension became theological data.

To earlier leaders, Greek and Roman texts in Christian schooling could seem very unsafe. Pope Gregory (c. 540–604) once called down shame on a bishop and requested the bishop to stop wasting time teaching the classical authors.

Yet Christians depended on Greek literacy to understand the Scripture. Better knowledge of Greek yielded insights to Scripture's meaning. Sometimes the pursuit of the meaning of a Scripture passage could lead to a Greek or Roman author. Christians were obliged to use teaching tools developed by pagans. The use of pagan learning could take trivial forms. The old standard Roman textbook of the rudiments of Latin—Donatus's *Ars Minor*—was updated with Bible names instead of those from mythology or classical history after the fifth century.

---

[16] Edwin Hatch, *The Influence of Greek Ideas on Christianity* (London: Williams and Norgate, 1891), 1–2; Jaeger, *Early Christianity and Greek Paideia*, 16.

In the end, Christian writings could not be quarantined from other Greek writings. Bonaventure (1221–1274), the monk-theologian-philosopher, could claim forcefully that "without practical knowledge of other sciences the Holy Scriptures cannot be understood"—echoing Augustine of Hippo. Over the centuries, the pursuit of a reasoning faith won out.[17]

KNOWLEDGE OF WORDS

The third continuing attribute of cloistered education was a tendency to formal or abstract education rather than practical. Schooling's prized outcome became the ability to engage in "critical thinking." With it, one could imagine a world different from the given one. Even practical professions today such as nursing, business, or teaching intellectualize their professional knowledge. Present-day secondary schools in North America and Europe encourage only the "less able" students toward hands-on vocational learning. Ability to manipulate mental structures is prestigious knowledge for Westerners. Abstraction was prized in the cloistered period. Why was abstraction held so highly?

First, Christians believed that God created the world by words. Indeed, the ultimate Word of God is God the Son. The earliest thinkers who prized the words of Scripture could propel their concern to extremes. Some read Scripture's words as if they were a code that could give special knowledge meant only for initiates. Jewish Kabbalists later computed numbers of letters to get special meanings from Scripture. In the same way, some Christians took a mystical approach to interpretation. The foundation of their understanding was the divinely given quality of scriptural words, but language mirrors the world. Less positively, words came to possess a reality of their own.[18]

Second, words name reality. God the Creator created categories as well as things. He did not only create individual items. After

---

[17] Orme, *Medieval Schools*, 29; Adamson, "Education," 256.
[18] Durkheim, *The Evolution of Educational Thought*, 47–49, 55–56.

all, the first human gave names to the animals (Gen. 2:19–20). God created the category of tables. A table is one of the genus "tables," a flat surface with legs. Crucially for medievals, God also created universal qualities. A white table is both white and a table. Naturally, the empirical "particulars," such as a table, are "real." They possess existence. But is the universal attribute, the adjective— the quality of whiteness—also real? This question was strongly debated.

Charlemagne (742–814), emperor of the vast central European "Holy Roman Empire," brought the monk and teacher Alcuin (c. 732–804) from northern England to help develop a Palace School— a school that would include nobles as well as those preparing for church careers.

Charlemagne's era was the "age of grammar." His educators were concerned above all to develop persuasive speaking ability. For rhetorical ability, the liberal arts were as indispensable as they had been to Greco-Roman education, particularly the *trivium* of grammar, rhetoric, and logic. Yet the age of grammar also set the foundations of the university three centuries later. Study of grammar led on to study of its structure, coordinating the mechanical rules of language to explain them into logic and dialectics.[19]

Driven by a desire to understand words and the Word of God, Alcuin wrote a sophisticated grammar. His grammar made no distinction between nouns and adjectives for just this reason—both the entity and its universals (its attributes) have substance. To him, both were realities.

Realism clarifies church teaching and goes well with certain truths such as the Trinity. However, realism raises problems too. Concepts such as how sin is transmitted from parents to child, the church entity, and the efficacy of sacraments hinged on a correct

---

[19] Durkheim, *The Evolution of Educational Thought*, 57–62; Samuel IJsseling, *Rhetoric and Philosophy in Conflict: An Historical Survey* (Dordrecht and London: Springer, 1976), 46.

understanding of the "reality of qualities" or "universals." In a Christian society, new knowledge that seemed to contradict revealed truth presented a huge problem.

The debate on "universals" reveals the basic impulse behind the developing educational movement. Education desired to integrate faith and knowledge. Since the human mind potentially reflects reality, it was important to erase wrong impressions. Detailed examination of grammar opened into the study of formal logical systems. Greek philosophy had seen discussion or dialectic as a main way to get at the whole truth of a proposition. Most of the varied achievements of Greek classical culture were remembered at least in some corners of medieval society.

Third, Christians believed in words because the knowledge of God was in two inspired books. The Bible is the first book of revelation, but the second is all around us (the created world). The sole Creator left a book of nature waiting to be read. The Artificer of the world left marks of his orderly ways all over his artifice. True knowledge of the physical world must therefore represent a second book about God. Naturally, the second book will never contradict the first one. The verbal book enables a reader to understand the world.

Fourth, Christians believed in words because the created human mind could connect the "books" of revelation and nature by grammar. To modern ears, the fine details of grammar and logic in medieval education come across as intellectual gamesmanship. But, if language bridges the created world to human beings, then understanding grammar is a way of understanding how the mind puts things together. To lay hold of what one is doing in formulating a sentence is to externalize the mind. Tracing grammar was thus working out what modern people call "an educational psychology." To medieval thinkers, the human mind potentially copies the physical world. Like wax taking the imprint of a seal, the mind takes the shape of the world. Grammar reflected the mind at work.[20]

Systematic logical review assured students of the truth of what was believed. One reasoned to gain a whole picture. Truth about the natural world came from reliable authorities. Arts students assimilated works of Boethius, Cicero, Peter of Spain, Isidore of Seville. The students of law, medicine, or theology appropriated their own authors. Areas of knowledge where Aristotle diverged from Christian truth, his *Ethics* or *Metaphysics*, were taught only in the higher faculties with reservations and qualifications explained by the instructor. From authoritative works, one reasoned to gain a whole picture. The drive to integration impelled higher schooling toward elaborate systems of logic.[21]

The pursuit of integrated knowledge of God's world together with the oral orientation of the teaching profession meant that verbal challenges were the most characteristic educational exercise. Characteristic concerns of medieval education, like its passion for public investigation of truth by disputation, were present from the earliest period. In debate, truth could win out. Errors would be exposed. Logic gained full use.[22]

It would be a mistake to think of the medieval society as static. Reason challenged faith. Faith sought integration. The pattern of reasoning developed by cloistered education brought classical rhetoric and philosophy as handmaids to the authority of Scripture. Pierre Abelard, a scholar and master (1079–1142), was a star of his time precisely because he pushed the boundaries of reason and faith—a central anxiety of his culture. A restless desire to integrate Scripture and experience gave a sense of danger to even the familiar question about the size of angels relative to a pin.

---

[20] Durkheim, *The Evolution of Educational Thought*, 57–62.
[21] IJsseling, *Rhetoric and Philosophy in Conflict*, 49–53; Durkheim, *The Evolution of Educational Thought*, 58.
[22] Adamson, "Education," 279.

The pattern of reasoning developed by faith seeking under-standing—though not its scriptural basis of authority—ironically carried over to the scientific era. Cloistered education was care-ful to follow a legal pattern of reason, giving the highest place to written words, chiefly about God, the Giver of the ultimate Word. Scientific thinking also followed the legally inspired pattern of rea-son, with high place to written words, though it replaced the divine authorization with the authority of autonomous thinking. The pri-ority of abstractions for education started in cloistered education, now equally important to modern empirical education.[23]

CATHEDRAL SCHOOL TO UNIVERSITY

After Charlemagne, cathedral schools developed at urban centers. Monastery schools continued to accept future monks, but cathe-dral schools began accepting not only future priests but also future professors, lawyers, and administrators.

Students began to seek out well-reputed masters. These might be found in Paris, for example, in a neighborhood on the left bank of the Seine River. Abelard taught in the bishop's cloister near Notre Dame Cathedral. The guilds of teaching masters were not neces-sarily centrally located. One reason that Oxford or Cambridge de-veloped masters' guilds was precisely because they were sufficiently remote from church authorities. Being distant from the bishop made it harder for him to interfere. Oxford and Cambridge were some distance from their cathedrals. Paris masters frequently tussled with their local church authorities. Academics tended to believe that their specialized work required qualified handlers. Church authorities were subject to institutional pressures and might confuse academic knowledge.

Organizations of masters developed all over Europe. Consor-tia of teachers were formally organized as universities in the 1100s. The medieval name for a corporation was simply "universitas."

---

[23] IJsseling, *Rhetoric and Philosophy in Conflict*, 52.

Universities were teacher's guilds. A bachelor's degree was the part-way qualification of an apprentice. A master's degree meant one was now included in the guild. It allowed the holder to serve as a master—that is, a professor. Bologna in northern Italy was an exception to this developing norm as a student guild formed to hire (and fire) its professors. Universities became perpetual institutions because when masters moved or died, their faculties sought replacements. The institutions continued.[24]

In 1291, the pope overruled interfering bishops and granted the guilds at Bologna and Paris the right to bestow degrees that were valid anywhere in Europe. The pope effectively agreed with the masters and gave them academic freedom from local church interference. The pope's license created the university as a distinctive European Christian institution. Academic freedom now allowed universities to go wherever truth seemed to lead, without pushback from church officials. Together, the two developments are cornerstones of Western education. They make the university the major contributor to the modernized world.[25]

In Paris, colleges assisting the work of a university developed by the late 1200s. Boys as young as twelve or thirteen years old pursued a university education. Secondary schools did not yet exist. The out-of-town students needed housing and food. After universities developed, colleges developed as charitable institutions and began to take on teaching functions as well.

Paris records show that many boys under the age of thirteen were pursuing Latin studies under the supervision of a college master. Latin ability was a prerequisite to university admission, since the scholarly lectures were in Latin and based on commentaries of authorities, also in Latin. In this accelerated education, eighteen- or twenty-year-olds could gain the master's degree.

---

[24] Durkheim, *The Evolution of Educational Thought*, 77–79.

[25] Alan B. Cobban, *The Medieval English Universities: Oxford and Cambridge to 1500* (Aldershot, UK: Scholar Press, 1988), 61.

Thirteen-year-olds, and even younger students, studied the logic in Aristotle's *Organon*.

To pass on this knowledge to such young students, teachers simplified it, and then simplified it again. The youthfulness of students drove a reduction of knowledge. Faculties fostered learning together, and people began to view knowledge more as a consortium property than as that of any one master. Teaching procedures that were likely to succeed became a series of deliberate steps. However, growing numbers in a now-corporate entity made personal influence on a student less important than systematic teaching of content.

Large numbers of students taught by a consortium of teachers brought another innovation. The master's degree conveyed the right to teach. Before this point, the final test for a license to teach was just one thing—demonstrated teaching success in debate. With the development of colleges and universities, students who kept up with the work and did not drop out could expect to gain a degree. The personal test of a debate now gave way to examinations in standardized, reproducible, testable knowledge.[26]

SUMMARY OF CLOISTERED EDUCATION

Cloistered education could answer Spencer's question, "What knowledge is of most worth?" without hesitation. In this tradition, the knowledge of most worth was knowledge of God, won by close attention to his words in Scripture and his word in the book of nature. The fact that cathedrals sponsored schools for boys to train them to sing in the choir illustrates that "knowledge of most worth" was a main force determining what schools taught.

Raymond Williams summarizes how the choice of subjects and disciplines develops a society:

---

[26] Walter J. Ong, *Ramus, Method, and the Decay of Dialogue: From the Art of Discourse to the Art of Reason* (Chicago: University of Chicago Press, 2005), 131–67.

It is not only that the way in which education is organized can be seen to express, consciously and unconsciously, the wider organization of a culture and a society, so that what has been thought of as simple distribution is in fact an active shaping to particular social ends. It is also that the content of education, which is subject to great historical variation, again expresses . . . certain basic elements in the culture, what is thought of as "an education"; being in fact a particular selection, a particular set of emphases and omissions.[27]

However, cloistered education's focus on words overtook the more personal knowledge mediated by the biblical narrative. As the historian of ideas Hatch noticed, philosophical abstraction blunted the salvation narrative. Getting the knowledge logically correct became an obsession. Cloistered education's passion for disputation serves as a graphic illustration of this common misstep.

- The culture's **Memory** was the Christian succession at Rome, a tradition increasingly modified by classical sources. The growth of their civilization from low levels after Roman withdrawal to a renaissance of learning in the 1100s seemed to confirm their confidence. Most Christians believed that their cultural efforts were contributing to the eventual visible reign of Christ—a postmillennial understanding of social progress culminating in the advent of the heavenly city.
- Christian Europe's **Vision** saw itself bringing in the reign of Christ on earth.
- **Symbols** such as the celtic cross with its orb centered on the middle indicated the victory of God at Easter and Christ the center of history.
- The culture's **Ethos** was a patchwork of pre-Christian practices increasingly dominated by Christian norms.

Cloistered education was perfectly suited to a hierarchical society. The world was ordered in a great chain of being running from

---

God to pope and kings to priests, monks, and clerks, to common men and women, and finally to animate and inanimate forms of life. Though dissidents could be found to raise their questions, Catholic European society shared an understanding of the purpose of life that gave its education the same hierarchical purpose. Cloistered education fitted its time and place.[28]

---

[28] Adamson, "Education," 284.

5

EMPIRICAL EDUCATION

1800–PRESENT

Modern-era public schools and major universities educate Christians in secular knowledge for secular aims. In Europe, Australia, and elsewhere, state-sponsored schools provide comparative religious education to all pupils. "Confessional" education is found only in private schools run by a church. In North America, specifically Christian education comes through church organizations and families. In all these cases, religious knowledge is deemed to be private knowledge and therefore separated from publicly accepted knowledge.

Four new approaches form schooling in the modern era. The new approaches are: (1) a shift in knowledge to empiricism; (2) in organization of learning to utilitarianism; (3) in administration toward efficiency; (4) from direction by religious bodies (usually) to direction by governments. These four commitments developed an education perfectly suited for a society in which religion is deemed a private matter, and in which economic advance is the overriding priority.

EDUCATION BY METHOD

The term *science* can denote a method for gaining reliable knowledge. Currently the *Shorter Oxford Dictionary* describes the most common use as "the intellectual and practical activity encompassing those branches of study that apply objective scientific method to the phenomena of the physical universe . . . and the knowledge so gained." Scientific method varies by scientific discipline—methods in biology differ from methods in chemistry. However, the sciences share a core procedure: carefully observe some aspect of nature; propose possible explanations; then, test the explanations. The Latin word, *scientia*, means simply, knowledge.[1]

The pursuit of methodical ways to know things arguably started with an educational problem in the early 1500s. Before the era in which secondary schools developed, a university student could be as young as thirteen. University was a student's next step after Latin language and literature. Universities required young students to study logic (also called dialectic). But logic was complicated and detailed. Peter Ramus, a Paris professor, wrote that only two hundred of the thousand or more students of his university who went to hear the professors were old enough to profit from the lectures.[2]

To meet students on their level, Ramus simplified logic. His textbooks organized logic so it could be easily assimilated. His books were reprinted all over Europe, so that many if not most intellectual leaders were influenced by his approach.

At least a hundred years before the pioneering modern philosopher Rene Descartes (1596–1650) pursued his famous search for a sure method of knowing—the search that led him to insist that sure knowing required geometrically clear, distinct ideas—Europeans pursued methodical knowledge.[3]

---

[1] Lesley Brown and William R. Trumble, eds., "Science," *Shorter Oxford English Dictionary* (Oxford: Oxford University Press, 2002), 2698; Stephen Carey, *A Beginner's Guide to Scientific Method* (Boston: Nelson Education, 2011), 5; Hugh G. Gauch, *Scientific Method in Practice* (Cambridge University Press, 2003), 5; Barry Gower, *Scientific Method: A Historical and Philosophical Introduction* (Routledge, 2012), 6.

[2] Walter J. Ong, *Ramus, Method, and the Decay of Dialogue: From the Art of Discourse to the Art of Reason* (Chicago: University of Chicago Press, 2005), 136.

[3] Ong, *Ramus, Method, and the Decay of Dialogue*; Stephen Petrina, Franc Feng, and Yu-Ling Lee, "On the Historiography of Curriculum: The Legend of Petrus Ramus" (annual meeting of the American Educational Research Association, Washington, DC, 2016) takes rare exception to Ong's history, which has remained authoritative; David Hamilton, "Instruction in the Making: Peter Ramus and the Beginnings of Modern Schooling" (annual meeting of the American Educational Research Association, Chicago, April 21, 2003); Elizabethanne Boran, "Ramus in Trinity College, Dublin in the Early Seventeenth Century," in *The Influence of Petrus Ramus: Studies in Sixteenth and Seven-*

The Scientific Revolution of the 1500s and 1600s changed ideas of sure knowledge completely. Astronomical discoveries by Copernicus, Brahe, Kepler, Galileo, and Newton led to new understandings of motion. Their work birthed modern physics, chemistry, and other sciences. The Scientific Revolution changed the human understanding of the universe; it changed the way humans understand themselves too.

An educator inspired by the Scientific Revolution was John Locke (1632–1704)—philosopher, political thinker, educator, and friend of Sir Isaac Newton (1642–1727), the famous physicist. Locke described himself modestly as an "under-laborer" who aimed to clear away doctrinal and philosophical overlays.

Locke was optimistic about education's power in his book *Some Thoughts Concerning Education* (1693). He wrote, "Of all the men we meet with, nine parts of ten are what they are, good or evil, useful or not, by their education. It is that which makes the great difference in mankind." The blank slate can be inscribed for good or for ill. Humans, he inferred, must be born without inborn ideas.[4]

For Locke, the best educational procedure was the same method that brought in the Scientific Revolution. Knowledge came not from words but directly from the things themselves. He wished to limit sure knowledge to what the five senses affirmed to be true. If (a) knowledge comes only from stimuli in the environment that is tasted, touched, heard, seen, or smelled, then (b) the mind, or the soul, must start as a blank slate. If the human mind comes unfurnished or unbiased, then (c) persons will learn best by studying things directly.

Locke's beliefs were controversial: Christians had long believed that children were born with a sinful nature. To his contemporaries, Locke's belief in a blank slate seemed to undercut the doctrine of

teenth Century Philosophy and Sciences, ed. M. Feingold, J. S. Freedman, and W. Rother (Basel: Schwabe, 2001), 177–99.
[4] John Locke, quoted in G. H. Bantock, *Artifice and Nature, 1350–1765*, vol. 1, Studies in the History of Educational Theory (London: George Allen & Unwin, 1980), 214–50.

original sin. Further, earlier Christians understood that the human mind comprehended the world because the Creator created both. Made in God's image, human beings could understand things similarly to how God does. Neither of Locke's affirmations seemed to be religiously orthodox.[5]

Locke took the mind as a scientific object. His answer to "How do we know?" was "By the mind at work on sense impressions." Words—the darlings of universities, building blocks of rhetorical education—now had little value. Empiricism took truth directly from things without preconceived ideas. Learning was writing on a blank slate. It remains the basic commitment behind hands-on learning.

Charles Dickens illustrates empiricism's shrinking idea of knowledge. He satirizes fact-oriented education in his 1854 novel *Hard Times*. A school-keeper by the name of Thomas Gradgrind claims,

> "Now, what I want is Facts. Teach these boys and girls nothing but Facts. Facts alone are wanted in life. Plant nothing else, and root out everything else. You can only form the minds of reasoning animals upon Facts: nothing else will ever be of any service to them. This is the principle on which I bring up my own children, and this is the principle on which I bring up these children. Stick to Facts, sir!"
>
> The instructor knows all the children in the class by their number. "Girl number twenty . . . I don't know that girl. Who is that girl?"
>
> "Sissy Jupe, sir," explained number twenty, blushing, standing up, and curtseying.
>
> "Sissy is not a name," said Mr. Gradgrind. "Don't call yourself Sissy. Call yourself Cecilia."
>
> "It's father as calls me Sissy, sir," returned the young girl. . . .

Though her father is a horse trainer, Sissy is unable to define a horse. The schoolmaster calls on his favorite student by his name. Bitzer recites:

---

[5] John Arthur Passmore, *The Perfectibility of Man*, 3rd ed. (Indianapolis: Liberty Foundation, 2000), 246.

"Quadruped. Graminivorous. Forty teeth, namely twenty-four grinders, four eye-teeth, and twelve incisive. Sheds coat in the spring; in marshy countries, sheds hoofs, too. Hoofs hard, but requiring to be shod with iron. Age known by marks in mouth."

Gradgrind says, "Now girl number twenty, you know what a horse is."[6]

Gradgrind strips away "fancy" and metaphor to credit only impersonal knowledge. His idea of worthwhile knowledge is empirically validated knowledge—useful, that is, able to be manipulated for one's purposes. He reduces complexity to simple, testable propositions of mathematical clarity. In this way, recognized knowledge changed from a focus on words to a focus on things. Dickens's irony is that unless animals are machines, Bitzer's empirical knowledge is worthless. Lacking school knowledge but knowing horses, Sissy is the wiser pupil. Education adopted the apparently sure empirical knowledge of its society, in the process losing meaningful connection with life.

LEARNING, RATIONALLY ORGANIZED

The second innovation of modern-era schooling is the organization of learning.

The word *curriculum* is a Latin word that means a track, like a circular racecourse. For example, an introductory course in a school makes a path so a group of students gain competence in a discipline. The course is the same in every offering, year after year. The presence of a Latin word can lead one to think that educators from the ancient world understood their management of time like a defined, repeating track. But as we saw in previous chapters, such an assumption isn't correct.

---

[6] Charles Dickens, *Hard Times: For These Times (Orig Title)* (London: Bradbury & Evans, 1854); Paulette Kidder, "The Eclipse of Transcendence in Dickens' Hard Times" (Eric Voegelin Society, American Political Science Association, Chicago, September 2, 2004), http://www.lsu.edu/artsci /groups/voegelin/society/2004%20Papers/Kidder2004.shtml; "Martha Nussbaum on Dickens's Hard Times," *Philosophy and Literature* 33, no. 2 (2009): 417–26; Nele Pollatschek, "'Discard the Word Fancy Altogether!' Charles Dickens's Defense of Ambiguity in Hard Times," *Dickens Quarterly* 30, no. 4 (December 1, 2013): 278.

In fact, *curriculum* as an education term first appears in documents of Leiden University in 1582. It appears next at the University of Glasgow in 1633—surprisingly late dates. Which developments in education called forth the term *curriculum* into use? Why was the concept needed?[7]

One development calling for the word *curriculum* is that empirical "things" need more of a framework than do words. Cloistered education was studying recognized Christian and classical authorities. Had the cloister been asked about a "curriculum," they would have offered their collection of reliable books, which comprised the body of knowledge. The *what* of education was its content. Thus, the content of cloistered education explained and justified itself.

By contrast, a rationalizing process that desired methodical efficiency required a framework that could explain and justify its existence. Spelling out the method required, say, a written document.

A second development spurring an idea of curriculum was the example of printed books after the middle 1400s. Printed books organized knowledge. Their typesetting and formatting signal how the knowledge related and cohered to other subjects. A follower of Ramus such as Jan Amos Komensky (1592–1670) worked out an education that would be a typography of the mind, a "didachography." The education historian, David Hamilton observes that instead of paper, pupils were seen to have minds that could be impressed with the symbols of knowledge. Instead of a typeface, the class-books and the rest of the apparatus served to make a mental impression. The ink was the voice of the master, since it conveyed information from the books to the minds of the listener, and school discipline was the press that kept the pupils at their work and compelled them to learn.[8] Education was becoming methodical.

Alongside newly methodical curricula, the term *classes* also appeared. In 1762, the faculty of Glasgow University (again) made the

---

[7] David Hamilton, *Towards a Theory of Schooling* (London: Falmer Press, 1989), 43.
[8] Hamilton, "Instruction in the Making," 4–5; Bantock, *Studies in the History of Educational Theory*, 1:196–97.

decision to convert a single-room apartment to a "classroom." The record of the decision was the first written use of *classroom* in the English language. A *class* complements the idea of a curriculum.

Until the modern era, schools were not age-graded. A cloistered class for singing or reading could include several levels of accomplishment, like a present-day homeschool. The pattern continued throughout the period, so that by the late middle ages, a thousand or two thousand students were enrolled at a physically small school in a market town. A thousand students might be enrolled because not all were necessarily present at any one time. Pictures of schools from the same period depict boys around a master engaged in a variety of assigned tasks.

The historical association of classes and curriculum makes sense when one realizes that pre-modern schools were not age-grouped. Medieval schools could enroll much larger numbers of students than could ever fit in their building. Teachers gave pupils individual or small-group instruction and a clutch of assignments. Pupils did not remain at the school building for the day. The new educational term *classes* thus marked a new concern for efficient methods after the middle 1700s.[9]

Changed beliefs further fertilized the concept of classes. Optimistic beliefs about humanity gained strength in the scientific era. Thinkers began to argue that human beings possessed natural sympathies for one another. Shared moral sentiments meant that one student could help another to learn. The notion led to monitorial instruction, outlined in the early 1800s by Andrew Bell and Joseph Lancaster. Lancaster wrote, "If the number of boys studying the same lesson . . . should amount to six, their proficiency will be nearly doubled by being classed."[10] These educators were concerned for disadvantaged groups such as orphans. Bell and

[9] Hamilton, *Towards a Theory of Schooling*, 42–43.
[10] Joseph Lancaster, *Improvements in Education* (1806).

Lancaster separately developed peer-teaching schemes where age groups advanced together, with older peers as teachers.[11]

The trend of methodical education with standardized curriculum in age-graded classes came to its logical culmination in 1848. John Philbrick, superintendent of education for Quincy, Massachusetts, developed a school of four stories and twelve classrooms, each with fifty-six pupils. His egg-crate school was copied everywhere. With a methodical curriculum, efficient classes, and optimum physical design, the school of the modern era had arrived.[12]

As a new field of curriculum studies developed, utilitarianism provided its assumptions. *Utilitarianism* is a political and economic philosophy intended to direct a society's choices. In utilitarian thinking, the rightness or wrongness of an action depends on whether it maximizes pleasure and minimizes pain. Utilitarians such as Jeremy Bentham (1748–1832) proposed that individuals are motivated by the greatest "utility." Therefore, society should aim to maximize pleasure and minimize pain for most persons.

In the utilitarian tradition, Herbert Spencer, a popular and prolific philosopher in Victorian England, developed a grand synthetic philosophy. Education was among his many projects. Writing when public education was being established, his book *Education: Intellectual, Moral, and Physical* was reprinted more than thirty-five times—an unacknowledged classic of the time. In "What Knowledge Is of Most Worth," Spencer writes,

> How to live? that is the essential question for us. Not how to live in the mere material sense only, but in the widest sense. . . .

---

[11] Hamilton, *Towards a Theory of Schooling*, 81; David Hogan, "The Market Revolution and Disciplinary Power: Joseph Lancaster and the Psychology of the Early Classroom System," *History of Education Quarterly* 29, no. 3 (1989): 381; Carl F. Kaestle, *Joseph Lancaster and the Monitorial School Movement: A Documentary History* (New York: Teachers College Press, 1973); John Franklin Reigart, *The Lancasterian System of Instruction in the Schools of New York City* (New York: Teachers College, Columbia University, 1916); Sir Adolphus William Ward and Alfred Rayney Waller, eds., "Education, § 17: Bell and Lancaster," in *The Victorian Age, Part Two*, vol. XIV, The Cambridge History of English and American Literature in 18 Volumes (1907–21) (London: The Macmillan Company, 1933).

[12] Hamilton, *Towards a Theory of Schooling*, 35–55.

In what way to treat the body; . . . in what way to manage our affairs . . . in what way to utilize all those sources of happiness which nature supplies.[13]

Spencer's education naturally focused on a sequence of activities useful for present-day society. God is only a glimmer on the horizon, and religion is listed with leisure.

Franklin Bobbitt, the first modern-era curriculum theorist, took Spencer's cue. He specified thousands of fine-grained aims for pupils in *How to Make a Curriculum* (1924). Bobbitt imagines a curriculum that covers vocational skills, personal hygiene, and religious life. Along with "ability to read and interpret facts expressed by commonly used types of graphs, diagrams, and statistical tables," he includes "ability to care properly for the feet" and "ability to make one's sleep contribute in maximum measure to the development and maintenance of a high level of physical vitality."

With Bobbitt, as with Spencer, schooling now includes every aspect of daily life. Bobbitt presents his curriculum as scientific, but his recommendations depend on values that he does not make explicit. Like Locke and Spencer, he assumes that present society is ideal. A curriculum can right any "shortcomings." Utilitarian curriculum is radical, in the sense that it returns to roots, but it is also deeply conservative because it thinks that present-day society is a good aim for people. Bobbitt's knowledge of most worth—like Spencer's—is not transcendent knowledge. Society was now pursuing a new ultimate aim of economic advancement. Its education naturally advanced it.[14]

Research in the new discipline of psychology also pushed curriculum in a utilitarian direction. Classical educators taught

---

[13] Herbert Spencer, "What Knowledge Is of Most Worth?," in *Education: Intellectual, Moral, and Physical* (New York: Hurst and Company, 1862), 18.

[14] Herbert Kliebard, "The Rise of the Scientific Curriculum and Its Aftermath," in *The Curriculum Studies Reader*, ed. David J. Flinders and Stephen J. Thornton (New York: Routledge, 2004), 40–41; Elliot W. Eisner, "Franklin Bobbitt and the 'Science' of Curriculum Making," *School Review* 75, no. 1 (Spring 1967): 34.

subjects because they believed them to build general mental ability. Plato promoted geometry for its general benefits for clear thinking. Schools taught languages or mathematics because of their value as mental disciplines. Now, education professor Edward L. Thorndike (1874–1949) contradicted the ancient reasoning of education. He showed that students who completed courses in geometry were no better at solving logical problems than were students who had not taken geometry. Thorndike also said that students could apply school learning only to identical elements found outside schooling, a principle he called "transfer of learning." Traditional curriculum began to lose much of its justification. Research thus augmented the utilitarian tendency of Bobbitt and the taxonomies.[15]

Benjamin Bloom's *Taxonomy of Educational Objectives: The Classification of Educational Goals* was a methodical step from Spencer and Bobbitt. It detailed a hierarchy of cognitive aims. After the first level (knowledge), each level included the previous level. Thus, the sixth, ultimate level achieved evaluation.

The 1964 companion volume listed a hierarchy of affective aims. Revised taxonomies based on Bloom appeared as recently as 2006. Bloom and co-authors

> organized cognitive processes into a one-way hierarchy, leading readers to conclude that knowledge is always a simpler behavior than comprehension, comprehension a simpler behavior than application, application a simpler behavior than analysis, and so forth through synthesis and evaluation.[16]

---

[15] D. C. Phillips and Jonas F. Soltis, *Perspectives on Learning*, 5th ed. (New York: Teachers College Press, 2009), 75–80; Ralph W. Tyler, "The Five Most Significant Curriculum Events in the Twentieth Century," *Educational Leadership* 44, no. 4 (1987): 36–37; Eisner, "Franklin Bobbitt," 32.

[16] Benjamin S. Bloom, *Taxonomy of Educational Objectives: The Classification of Educational Goals, Handbook I: Cognitive Domain* (New York and London: Longman's, Green and Co., 1956); David R. Krathwohl, Benjamin S. Bloom, and Bertram B. Masia, *Taxonomy of Educational Objectives, Handbook II: The Classification of Educational Goals, Handbook II: Affective Domain* (New York and London: Longman Group Ltd., 1964); Richard W. Paul, "Bloom's Taxonomy and Critical Thinking Instruction," *Educational Leadership* 42, no. 8 (1985): 39.

A taxonomy of "Goldilocks and the Three Bears" illustrates Bloom's empiricist thinking:

> **Remember:** describe where Goldilocks lived.
> **Understand:** summarize what the Goldilocks story was about.
> **Apply:** construct a theory as to why Goldilocks went into the house.
> **Analyze:** differentiate between how Goldilocks reacted and how you would react in each story event.
> **Evaluate:** assess whether or not you think this really happened to Goldilocks.
> **Create:** compose a song, skit, poem, or rap to convey the Goldilocks story in a new form.[17]

The taxonomies led North American teacher candidates to think about teaching *empirically*, that is, based on knowledge from the senses. Empiricism, specifically behaviorism, dominated the period. Harvard psychology researcher B. F. Skinner's programmed learning similarly led teachers to imagine a simple-to-complex process. Arts educator Elliot Eisner observes that Bloom's taxonomy is "no mere classification scheme. It was an effort to hierarchically order cognitive processes."[18]

Bloom-style learning theory was not the only possible way to understand learning. A simple-to-complex process, or concrete-to-abstract, depended on empiricist assumptions. Bloom depended on unseen assumptions. By contrast, in narrative forms of learning, as in fairy stories, children grasped complex situations of good and evil. Empiricist learning was a natural choice in scientific societies—but not the only possible choice.[19]

---

[17] Anonymous, "Comprehension: Bloom's Taxonomy," *Teacher's Corner, Omaha Public Schools* (blog), accessed June 20, 2017, http://www.ops.org/reading/blooms_taxonomy.html via archive.org (first archived Dec. 17, 1999).

[18] Elliot W. Eisner, "Benjamin Bloom: 1913–1999," *Prospects* 30, no. 3 (2000): 389.

[19] Kieran Egan, *Primary Understanding: Education in Early Childhood* (London: Routledge, 1988), 15–26, 190.

EFFICIENT EDUCATION

The third new approach that brought modern schooling was the concern that narrow knowledge needed to be delivered efficiently.

Emerging education systems in scientific, industrial, highly organized societies adopted the rationalized management of industry. Prussia, France, Holland, and other European states had national education schemes by the early 1800s. In the United States, massive immigration after 1830 brought millions of new pupils into urban education systems every decade. Attendance had become mandatory. In the two decades between 1879 and 1898, school enrolment more than doubled, from seven million to fifteen million. After 1900, the city education systems of the young republic absorbed more than one million more students per year.

A bureaucratic education system naturally looked to industrial efficiency experts like Frederick W. Taylor and Frank Gilbreth for organizational know-how. By 1913, Henry Ford's miraculous moving assembly line of precisely made, interchangeable parts reduced production time for an automobile from 12 hours and 30 minutes to 5 hours and 50 minutes. Superintendents of education sought similar efficiencies. The historian Raymond Callahan's *Cult of Efficiency* gives an example. In *Laggards in Our Schools* (1909), author Leonard Ayres tracked the cost of pupils who repeated grades. With industrial reasoning, he urged that a system was wasting half its raw material if only half of pupils reach eighth grade; efficiency was only 50 percent. If System A briskly moved eight thousand students to the end of the line, while System B held a thousand students back one grade and carried nine thousand, inefficient System B was bearing unnecessary costs. Efficient teaching and testing procedures in the classroom could make an efficient system.[20]

Linking "business efficiency, American schooling, and the public school superintendency," one writer observed that

---

[20] Raymond E. Callahan, *Education and the Cult of Efficiency* (Chicago: University of Chicago Press, 1964), 18–19.

public education in the twentieth century had become a colossal business operation. In the face of this development, school superintendents must become business administrators. In one North Carolina county . . . "the superintendent of schools operated a public transportation system of greater magnitude than the state's largest city bus system . . . yet transportation was only one of the many business matters for which that superintendent was responsible."[21]

Expedited testing made for additional efficiency. To cut down on the time-consuming work of grading essays, "objective" tests checked reading ability. A 1915 article entitled "The Measurement of Efficiency in Reading" urged teachers to test pupils by giving exactly thirty seconds for each of eight graded passages. Comprehension or critical thinking could not be tested by word recognition, of course. In changing the test, the definition of valued learning became narrower. Knowledge now had to be reproducible in order to be recognized. Like empirical knowledge, such testing could seem arbitrary rather than meaningful.[22]

STATE EDUCATION

Ironically enough, state-sponsored schooling started in the Europe-wide Christian renewal movement known as the Protestant Reformation. Martin Luther, an Augustinian monk and university professor of Scripture, posted topics for debate (the famous 95 Theses) on the door of his parish church in 1517. In the two decades that followed Luther's challenge, European statelets and nations divided between those remaining loyal to Rome and those following

---

[21] Barbara Berman, "Business Efficiency, American Schooling, and the Public School Superintendency: A Reconsideration of the Callahan Thesis," *History of Education Quarterly*, 1983: 299; citing William H. Cartwright, "Education and the Cult of Efficiency: A Study of the Social Forces That Have Shaped the Administration of the Public Schools. By Raymond E. Callahan (Chicago: University of Chicago Press, 1962)," *Journal of American History* 49, no. 4 (March 1, 1963): 722–23.

[22] JoBeth Allen, "Taylor-Made Education: The Influence of the Efficiency Movement on the Testing of Reading Skills" (US Department of Education, Eric Document Reproduction Service, No. ED 239 247, June 1984), ERIC; Jonathan Rees, "Frederick Taylor in the Classroom: Standardized Testing and Scientific Management," *Radical Pedagogy* 10 (2001).

Lutheran or Calvinist understanding of Scripture. For Protestant states, a vital question was how to maintain the renewal.

The answer was educational and political. Since reading the Scriptures contributed strongly to the renewal, nobility and governments put new emphasis on literacy. Boys would be future leaders, and girls would be shapers of the next generation in the home. However, Luther had little confidence in parents' ability to teach their own children well. "The common man can do nothing. He doesn't have the means for it, he doesn't want to do it, and he doesn't know how," wrote Luther in 1524. Two years later he wrote to urge his prince to be "a guardian-general of the young," and in 1530 endorsed compulsory school attendance. A historian summarizes: "Reformation church and Reformation state seized upon the control of schooling as an efficient and effective way of acting directly on individual subjects for the purpose of instilling in them a lasting sense of their places and duties in the well-ordered society." The Reformation could be maintained if coming generations were educated.[23]

It turned out that state-sponsored education could leave its church behind. Until the French Revolution of 1789, Europe understood that a national church body and the national mechanisms of the state formed a society together. An established single church, whether of the Protestant variety or Catholic, kept religious education in most schools of most countries. After the French Revolution, however, Napoleon sponsored government education. He had his reasons—government sponsorship could encourage an integrated French polity not conflicted with other (religious) loyalties. France formalized state-run education in 1833. Other European countries copied the pattern, including Germany and Holland.[24]

[23] Gerald Strauss, "The Social Function of Schools in the Lutheran Reformation in Germany," *History of Education Quarterly* 28, no. 2 (1988): 193–95.

[24] Michalina Vaughan and Margaret Scotford Archer, *Social Conflict and Educational Change in England and France 1789–1848* (Cambridge: Cambridge University Press, 2010), 180–84; Regis Dericquebourg, "Religious Education in France," in *The Routledge International Handbook of*

In the US, the Massachusetts colony that Puritans founded in 1630 assigned legal responsibility for schools to its towns and villages. In 1837, Horace Mann became the secretary of a state-wide advocacy group, the Massachusetts Board of Education. The board had no schools. Its secretary and only employee commenced the work of building support for state-supported and directed schools. America's democracy was expanding to include voters without property, and urban immigration was adding non-Protestant, non-English-speaking future voters. Mann feared that widespread "false knowledge" would threaten order. His idea was "not that all men [sic], however unfit, shall be voters, but that every man, by the power of reason and the sense of duty, shall become fit to be a voter." He wanted state-sponsored schools to maintain democracy by educating citizens of wisdom and character. The proposed schools would teach the Bible without theological interpretation. They would teach a generic Christian morality, similar to Mann's own Unitarian faith. Calvinist sermons had repelled the youthful Mann. Where Protestant Germany at first educated to maintain the Protestant faith that maintained the state, Mann's public education aimed to maintain the civic religion that maintained the state.[25]

Mann's approach eventually divided the educational labor between schools and churches. But not right away. Throughout the 1800s, public schools expressed the establishment Protestant ethos. Prayer and Bible reading usually opened the day. Textbooks such as the widely used McGuffey Readers fused reading instruction with Protestant morality. In some jurisdictions, American public schools of the 1800s released students for denominational religious instruction time. Catholics came to see public schools as a hazard to their

---

Religious Education, ed. Derek Davis and Elena Miroshnikova (Abingdon, UK and New York: Routledge, 2013), 115.
[25] Gerald L. Gutek, *An Historical Introduction to American Education*, 3rd ed. (Long Grove, IL: Waveland Press, 2012), 10–14; James W. Fraser, *Between Church and State: Religion and Public Education in a Multicultural America*, 2nd ed. (Baltimore: JHU Press, 2016), 22; Michael J. Steudeman, "Horace Mann, 'The Necessity of Education in a Republican Government' (Fall 1839)," *Voices of Democracy* 8 (2013): 6.

faith—the schools were too religious, too Protestant. In 1884, the Catholic hierarchy urged all parishes to open a Catholic school. A parallel Catholic school system was the result, and at its peak enrolled almost half of the Catholic school-age population. On the Protestant side, a few strongly confessional groups objected to public education too: Mann's Christianity was not specific enough. A Presbyterian group attempted its own parochial schools. But Protestant dissenters were few, because public schools in their first century supported and reflected society's broadly Protestant values.[26]

By the 1970s, religious pluralism in Western democracies made confessional religious education impossible in public schools. A public school could include Protestants, Catholics, skeptics, atheists, possibly a Muslim or Buddhist. Human rights codes halted publicly funded institutions from teaching any one faith tradition as truth. State schooling in many countries of Western Europe continued to include religious education. However, religions were presented comparatively or as neutral phenomena. Schools did religion descriptively, not prescriptively. No belief system was taught as a reliable narrative about reality—except for scientific accounts. Religious education in Europe, and in Canada's province of Quebec, increasingly adopted the political aim of encouraging religious tolerance or reducing the risk of religiously inspired violence. In these jurisdictions, public schooling offered religious education as part of civics.

Empirical education said that empirical validation or scientific method determined reliable knowledge. Since religion wasn't science, religion was not reliable knowledge. Religious education was thus only development of an individual preference, not public

---

[26] Anne M. Boylan, *Sunday School: The Formation of an American Institution, 1790–1880* (New Haven, CT: Yale University Press, 1990), 58–59; Steven K. Green, *The Bible, the School, and the Constitution: The Clash That Shaped Modern Church-State Doctrine* (New York: Oxford University Press, 2012), 13–15; Timothy Walch, *Parish School: American Catholic Parochial Education from Colonial Times to the Present* (Crossroad Publishing, 1996), 32, 48; Stephen J. Denig and Anthony J. Dosen, "The Mission of the Catholic School in the Pre-Vatican II Era (1810–1962) and the Post-Vatican II Era (1965–1995): Insights and Observations for the New Millennium," *Journal of Catholic Education* 13, no. 2 (2009): 141.

truth. Religious knowledge was Spencer's last kind of worthwhile knowledge. In empirical education, religious education was for individuals; it was not to promote specific (orthodox Christian) beliefs in the population. Scientific education thus fenced in any religious contributions.[27]

CHURCHES RESPOND

Church-related Sunday schools grew as public education adopted Mann's generic moral Christianity. Originally formed in England to provide basic literacy and numeracy to poor children, Sunday schools in America brought the gospel to children in cities. The major organization was the American Sunday School Union, founded in 1824. It engaged missionaries to settlers in the new Western territories, became a major publisher, and established free libraries in urban areas. Its leaders were mostly not ordained clergy. The union was officially non-denominational. To maintain their distinctive perspectives in their Sunday schools, major denominations began publishing their own lessons and literature. They developed educational divisions with resource persons, conferences, and training to support educational efforts in their churches.

After the later decades of the 1800s, independent curriculum publishers discovered that assertions about race, prophecies, or topics such as predestination or human free will would turn a market segment against them. Their response was curriculum that repeated central, uncontroversial beliefs or made Scripture into moral lessons. Systematic theology articulated biblical meaning for a place and time. While curriculum avoided specific theologies because of their controversial applications of the Bible to the

---

[27] Christopher Dawson, *Education and the Crisis of Christian Culture* (Chicago: Regnery, 1949), 6; Warren A. Nord, *Does God Make a Difference?: Taking Religion Seriously in Our Schools and Universities* (New York: Oxford University Press, 2010); W. A. Nord, *Religion and American Education: Rethinking a National Dilemma* (Chapel Hill: UNC Press, 1995); Andrew Wright, *Religious Education and Postmodernity* (London: RoutledgeFalmer, 2003); Catherine Byrne, *Religion in Secular Education: What, in Heaven's Name, Are We Teaching Our Children?*, vol. 21, International Studies in Religion and Society (Leiden: Brill, 2014).

current culture, the content became vague. Without theology, cultural relevance was hard to achieve.[28]

Shallow materials and classes dismayed sensitive religious people. Founded in 1903, the Religious Education Association and its journal sought a professional and scientific religious education. General education for schools was professionalizing. The Religious Education Association advocated that church staffs add a Director of Religious Education. The aim was biblical, theological, and social literacy for laypersons. A parallel movement in conservative churches and seminaries developed for church-based Christian education after the conservative theological reactions in the mid-twentieth century. The religious education movement shifted responsibility for church education programs from the main clergy person to an assistant. As ideas of local church success shifted toward social activism or numerical growth, pastors met parishioners' expectations by doing more than Sunday preaching. Their role shifted from teaching. But, senior pastors were normally the theologically equipped individuals in the church and were also the most likely bridge to any improvements in lay education. Church-based directors of education proved unable to move congregations beyond Sunday schooling.[29]

SUMMARY OF EMPIRICAL EDUCATION

Empiricism split knowledge between knowledge of the world on one hand and knowledge of the self on the other. The split of world from self came at the beginning of the modern era when René Descartes, looking for a sure foundation of knowledge,

[28] Robert W. Lynn and Elliott Wright, *The Big Little School: Sunday Child of American Protestantism* (New York: Harper & Row, 1971); Joseph Bayly, "Evangelical Curriculum Development," *Religious Education* 75, no. 5 (1980): 539–45; James Wilhoit, "The Bible Goes to Sunday School: An Historical Response to Pluralism," *Religious Education* 82, no. 3 (1987): 395, 403–4.

[29] Edward Farley, "Can Church Education Be Theological Education?," *Theology Today* 42, no. 2 (July 1985): 158–71; Farley, "The Tragic Dilemma of Church Education" in *Caring for the Commonweal: Education for Religious and Public Life*, ed. Parker J. Palmer, Barbara G. Wheeler, and Robert W. Lynn (Atlanta: Mercer University Press, 1990); Dwayne Huebner, "Can Theological Education Be Church Education?," *Union Seminary Quarterly Review* 47 (1993).

claimed "I think, therefore I am" as sure knowledge of his own consciousness. He made himself sure of the reality of the external world by proofs of a good God who would not maliciously deceive him. When God's existence came into question in later centuries, sure knowledge of the external world also came into question. Empiricism could not postulate that human values are sure knowledge.

Scientific knowledge accounts for human self-awareness only with difficulty. In recent decades, neuroscience attempted to understand human behavior as scientific knowledge. It tended to see human responses to stimuli as similar to responses that all animals make in their environments to survive. But humans are conscious of their ability to make choices. We know ourselves as subjects. On one hand are scientific facts; on the other hand are human values.

An educational result of the scientific-human split is classroom knowledge that is unconnected to daily experience. The Brazilian literacy educator Paulo Freire (1927–1991) identified knowledge that lacked significance for personal and political life as "banking knowledge." By the term, he meant that teachers in schools urge pupils to learn for their futures, to bank knowledge that they will access later in careers. Knowledge presented this way makes it abstract, not relevant to the person in the here and now. Freire's radical solution was to design curriculum collaboratively with a group, starting from problems that students experience. His proposal "situates" learning. He responds to the split of science and human values that empiricism brings. "Banking" of impersonal knowledge is a predictable result when sensory things gain priority over meaning-laden narratives.

Empiricist education's rise made religious education increasingly marginal, both in time allotted during class time and through the physical locations of religious education. Social institutions such as schools were reorganized from the preceding

Christian society. The revised institutions expressed the still-increasing dominance of empirical knowledge in present-day societies. Agencies of specifically Christian education—family, church, seminary, Christian day school, Christian university—now carried on the work as a subculture. Religious education continued, but without the benefits and sanctions of the most influential shapers of a society.

In an influential analysis, Lutheran theologian Robert Jenson observed that the world lost its story. By this, he meant that the hope of the Scientific Revolution and the Enlightenment movement was a world that was not violently pushed and pulled by rival stories. The Thirty Years' War of the 1600s, really a series of Protestant-versus-Catholic regional wars, provided a powerful push toward Enlightened post-religions Europe. Science helped by depicting a world without a storyteller. After the violent disappointments of the twentieth century, however, postmodernism marked the end of the Enlightenment's hope. Jenson says that the challenge for churches and allied bodies now is to learn to retell the Christian story. Protestants especially gave up many of the ritual and symbolic ways in which the old church enacted the story. Renewed education—and initiation in general—demands storytelling that is more than simply head knowledge. The story must be told by meaningful actions—"gestures," as one theologian calls them.

- **Memory**: Though dogma and tradition made the West a violent, superstitious place, empirical science is gradually replacing it with a rational world ruled by science and laws. Religion's place can only be in private life, where it cannot interfere with public order.
- **Vision**: A shining city on a hill of rational men and women living in harmony with each other, fully dominating nature to reduce fear and chance to the barest minimum.
- **Symbols**: The rational metric system of measurement that replaced ad hoc traditional weights and measures; the public

school; elections to democratic systems peopled by basically good people; rationalized ways of governing such as bureauctratic procedures.

- **Ethos**: Scientific management of natural and human resources.

Education that understands the imperative of challenging the dominant scientific Memory, Vision, Symbols, and Ethos—parts of a holistic schema for life—is intensely relevant to recovering a lived Christian worldview.

6

PROGRESSIVE EDUCATION

1800–PRESENT

What is good teaching? Questions about good methods of teaching seem to be everywhere in mainstream education. For example, should learning be student-centered? Do a variety of learning styles exist? Does a distinct bodily-kinesthetic intelligence complement the familiar linguistic intelligence? How important is psychology of learning? Should university classes move from "objective" knowledge relayed by lectures toward student-centered approaches that enable students to construct knowledge? Current academic writing, online presentations, and teacher media take active learning techniques as high priorities.

These questions arise from the progressive movement in education. Development-oriented approaches emerged in the late 1800s. Forerunners include Jan Amos Komensky (1592–1670) and Jean-Jacques Rousseau (1712–1778). John Locke's emphasis on education that was useful for social life rather than "useless" classical education helped to pave the way.[1]

Progressive education based itself on a child's sense experiences, preferred over teacher (verbal) representations of the world. It proposed to make education as pleasant and painless as possible.

---

[1] Bernadette Baker, "The Dangerous and the Good? Developmentalism, Progress, and Public Schooling," *American Educational Research Journal* 36, no. 4 (1999): 797–834.

"Hands-on" is an appropriate slogan for a progressive way of teaching. Its priority for knowledge from personal experience orients it to the student's experience. It often centers on the subjective learning process of individuals, though writers in recent decades have made more allowance for shared language and communal learning.

The basic commitment behind active learning was that persons gain justified beliefs by directly examining things. Its commitment to direct knowledge was that of *empiricism*. Genuine knowledge must come without the prejudices of dogmatic beliefs—the standard belief of the Enlightenment movement.

Progressive education's difference from empirical education is that the individual is the interpreter of knowledge, not the scientific community. The thinking, feeling, willing, whole person makes "meaning" by discovering knowledge. The pupil must subjectively appropriate a fact so that it matters to him.[2]

GRANDFATHER ÉMILE

Jean-Jacques Rousseau's book *Émile, or On Education*, published in 1762, reveals the basic issues that propel progressivism. France in the mid-1700s was home to Voltaire, Diderot, D'Alembert, and other popular intellectuals who heralded the demise of rigid religious control of society. To them, scientific reason opened a wide horizon of human potential.

Among "philosophes," Rousseau was a contrarian, the *enfant terrible* of the Enlightenment. His writings cast doubt that the society of his day could perfect civilization. Rousseau believed that by allowing property ownership, civilization forced insincere behavior. Hypocrisy alienated human beings from their true selves and from society. Social hypocrisy was Rousseau's equivalent to the Christian idea of inherited sin. Social relations of domination plague society,

---

[2] Immanuel Kant, *Foundations of the Metaphysics of Morals And, What Is Enlightenment* (Macmillan, 1990), 83–88.

a plague that has grown over time. Rousseau recovered Lucretius's materialist story of human origins to imagine how social decline commenced. The unfortunate course of history led human societies into misshapen form.[3]

Forming a new kind of society was Rousseau's overall project. His book *The Social Contract*, also published in 1762, described political arrangements for progress. He sought to reverse the long decline of society and attain progress in history.

Progressive education is therefore Rousseau's main means of redirecting history and remaking human societies. To Rousseau, Locke's empirical education would not result in ideal human beings but in uptight city dwellers who still depend on others for a sense of self-worth. *Émile* is Rousseau's thought experiment about one innocent human being who manages to begin to change history. Helped by his fictional tutor Rousseau, Émile avoids most social contact in order to retain his original innocence. Rousseau aims to restore Émile's true natural self by isolating him from the source of corruption—other people—until the teen years.

Émile must learn naturally as problems engage his interest. Unless a problem engages Émile, acquiring knowledge about it is a waste of time. Useless knowledge is useless education. The tutor's work is in designing situations so Émile will take interest and learn. The tutor does not actively teach but—using present-day terms—facilitates learning. An example of Émile's experiential learning comes when he breaks a window. After he experiences the resulting cold, he will not throw rocks at windows anymore. Similarly, by navigating his way out of a forest, Émile learns the value of mathematics.

By placing Émile in physical nature, his good, original human nature shines forth. Émile develops in three pre-adolescent stages, then two post-adolescent stages. In the pre-adolescent phases,

---

[3] Allan Bloom, "Introduction," in J. J. Rousseau, *Émile, or On Education*, trans. Allan Bloom (New York: Basic Books, 1979), 15.

Émile can keep his natural goodness by acting on things—by practical activities. Émile's tutor exhorts, "Remember always that the spirit of my education consists not in teaching the child many things, but in never letting anything but accurate and clear ideas enter his brain," so "continue to be clear, simple and cold."[4] Wordless things directly educate learners in the way empiricist scientists taught themselves to observe.

Émile can know the natural world not through words but through direct contact. Like Locke, Rousseau has little faith in words. "Young people pay little attention to them and hardly retain them. Things, things! I shall never repeat enough that we attribute too much power to words. With our babbling education we produce only babblers." However, Rousseau thinks Locke makes a major mistake in urging reasoning with the pupil. It is a waste because children do not think as adults do. Rousseau lists examples of a child's predictable misconceptions. He reads through LaFontaine's fable of the crow and the fox and sees that Émile will hopelessly misunderstand. Émile should not even learn to read until he is twelve. Contact with culture via texts will corrupt Émile. His one book is Daniel Defoe's *Robinson Crusoe* (1719)—the story of how one man survived well on an island, mostly by himself.[5]

Rousseau's fable ends with Émile as a true human being, and at the same time, a genuinely contributing citizen. He ends the strategy of isolating Émile at adolescence. He leads him to read and to engage in society. Grown up uncorrupted, Émile will hardly understand the motives of his civilized fellows. By "Stage Five," asocial Émile will join domestic life. Though male and female halves of human nature somehow came apart in history, love will reunite them perfectly. The sociality of a woman, plus a man true to his own nature, will make a harmonious whole. Rousseau's vision is biologically and socially complementarian.

---

[4] Rousseau, *Émile*, 171.
[5] Rousseau, *Émile*, 180.

Émile outlines the first modern theory of development. The ancient idea of development (paideia, for example) saw human beings formed into an ideal image by the content and disciplines of education. Rousseau sees stages of development. In the same way humans develop biologically from child to adult, they develop mentally. The stages do not vary. His education matches learning to Émile's stages of development. Refuting ancient wisdom, disciplined learning does not bring development. Any educative effort must accommodate the inevitable stages. Any content will do. Rousseau thus stood the older idea of development on its head.[6]

CHRISTIAN ROUSSEAUANS

Christians including J. H. Pestalozzi (1746–1827) and Friedrich Froebel (1782–1852) picked up the child-centered approach. Like Rousseau, Pestalozzi saw education as the means to a more just society, but he thought that Rousseau's education was too individualistic, not educating sufficiently for the wider community. True love loves other human beings before being directed to God. Since love is the only way to true humanness, Pestalozzi sought to replicate the parent's outgoing love in the child.[7]

Pestalozzi accepted Rousseau's insistence that direct contact with nature was the child's main teacher. Contact with nature will unfold innate human abilities. Teachers should add verbal labels to phenomena only after the child has sufficient experience.

> I wish to wrest education from the outworn order of doddering old teaching hacks as well as from the new-fangled order of cheap, artificial teaching tricks, and entrust it to the eternal powers of nature herself, to the light which God has kindled and kept alive in the hearts of fathers and mothers.

[6] Kieran Egan, "Students' Development in Theory and Practice: The Doubtful Role of Research," *Harvard Educational Review* 75, no. 1 (2005): 25–26.
[7] Clem Adelman, "Over Two Years, What Did Froebel Say to Pestalozzi?," *History of Education* 29, no. 2 (2000): 107.

Active learning slogans such as "from simple to complex," "from the known to the unknown," and "from concrete to abstract" stem from Pestalozzi's emphasis on empirical reality. Pestalozzi's moral Christianity imagines a good creation educating a basically good human being.[8]

Friedrich Froebel transformed Pestalozzi's system for his own educational concern. Froebel's scheme of directed play focused student learning on specially selected objects, which he called "gifts." Froebel's early university training was as a crystallographer who appreciated the geometric intricacy of God's works. By comprehending gifts such as sphere, cylinder, and cube, pupils develop skills of perception, manipulation, and combination. Froebel designed his educative process to lead pupils into a harmony of outward experience and inner consciousness. He sought religious, perhaps mystical, aims for education. Froebel desired that children learn the unity of experience as experience of God, to foster a model German society that the whole world could emulate. The designer of the first kindergarten was propelled by high aims. Like Pestalozzi, Froebel relied on the orderliness of creation to speak clearly about a good Creator.[9]

The theories of Rousseau, Pestalozzi, and Froebel reacted against science's division of scientific knowledge from human values. Rousseau and other subjectivists questioned any so-called knowledge that was without human connection.

Subjectivism's persistent problem, however, was whether one can be sure that a subject's knowledge is justified belief. Mainstream science claims to see truth objectively, without bias from the human subject's history, context, or beliefs. It brackets out the

---

[8] Quote is from Kate Silber, *Pestalozzi: The Man and His Work* (New York: Schocken Books, 1973), 136; Niko Kolodny, "The Explanation of Amour-Propre," *Philosophical Review* 119, no. 2 (April 1, 2010): 165–200; M. K. Smith, "Johann Heinrich Pestalozzi: Pedagogy, Education and Social Justice," *Infed.Org* (blog), 2014; Debora B. Agra Junker, "Pestalozzi, Johann Heinrich," ed. George T. Kurian and Mark A. Lamport, *Encyclopedia of Christian Education* (Lanham, Maryland: Rowman & Littlefield Publishers, 2015).

[9] Adelman, "Over Two Years"; "Play as a Quest for Vocation," *Journal of Curriculum Studies* 24, no. 2 (March 1, 1992): 139, notes that neither educator relied on the child's innate innocence for their actual practices.

human element. Rousseau and those who follow him have split knowledge on the other side. They have the human being and relevance but not the apparent certainty. Focused on human values and the subject, progressivism gained the student but lost the world.

John Dewey (1859–1952), probably America's most influential philosopher, saw education as the seedbed of democratic society. Founder of the University of Chicago's experimental school, he wrote *The School and Society* (1900), *The Child and the Curriculum* (1902), and *Democracy and Education* (1916), among others. Each of the titles indicated two entities. The books explore their relationship. Dewey understood his work as repairing the division of science and self. Action of one side (say, the child) and (the curriculum) on the other would bring resolution. The subjective child brought the sides to a living unity by acting and reacting on the knowledge of the curriculum. Humans only "know" as they act on objects. Dewey did not believe in unchanging truth. He thought truths depend on their era. Science changes. Humans only know what works—technically stated, what proves fruitful in generating further knowledge. Dewey's truth was relativistic. Ultimate knowledge was beyond subjects who were limited to a time and a place. Subjects in a society accordingly construct "knowledge" together by means of language. Since democracy was a striving, forward-looking way of life that people engaged in together, education—and public schooling—was the basic institution of democracy.

Progressive expressions in education include A. S. Neill's Summerhill School in East Anglia, England, where pupils attend classes only when they desire it. Like Émile, learning must be intrinsically motivated. Neill's education does not necessarily depend on submitting to a school's discipline. At Summerhill, students together set consequences for anti-social behavior. Other progressive educators include Paulo Freire, Ivan Illich, John Dewey, Maria Montessori, Jean Piaget, and Lev Vygotsky, to name a few. Dedicated schools in their tradition function in locales worldwide. Their larger influence is in practices inserted into empirical education. Government departments of education insist on accountability for definite bodies of knowledge in each year of schooling, on the empirical model. Progressive techniques help to maintain pupil motivation while modifying empiricist practices.

Progressive Christians welcomed Dewey, who was a founder of the Religious Education Association (1903). Conservatives struggle with an open-ended conception of truth. God revealed himself progressively over history, to be sure, but biblical truth is not open-ended. God providentially directs history. For Christians, history arrives at a definite full truth: God's glory in Christ, the divinely revealed center of history and end-point of creation. Dewey's pragmatic philosophy raises theological questions.

HOW TO THINK PROGRESSIVELY

Constructivism in education emphasizes that pupils strive to construct a picture of reality for themselves. Twentieth-century constructivists include Jean Piaget, Lev Vygotsky, Ernst von Glasersfeld, and Howard Gardner. Each theorist relies on a set of philosophical assumptions. An example is Piaget's biological version of Kant's knowledge categories. To Piaget, individual subjects develop capacities for learning in marked stages reminiscent of Rousseau's five stages. Some constructivists are more concerned that the child's reality should match the way the world is. Some are less concerned. An extreme example is Glasersfeld, a skeptic who believes independently verifiable knowledge of reality is impossible.[10]

An example of constructivism's attraction was Gardner's multiple intelligences. Gardner's expanded ways of knowing includes linguistic knowing (using vocabulary, playing with words, and applying metaphors), logico-mathematical knowing (manipulating

---

[10] Ernst von Glasersfeld, "An Exposition of Constructivism: Why Some Like It Radical," in *Constructivist Views on the Teaching and Learning of Mathematics*, ed. Robert Davis, Nel Noddings, and Carolyn Mahar, vol. 4, *Journal for Research in Mathematics Education Monograph* (Reston, VA: National Council of Teachers of Mathematics, 1990), 19–29.

numbers and symbols), but also musical knowing, spatial knowing (perceiving and reproducing the visual world), bodily-kinesthetic knowing (awareness and control of one's body), and a seventh, intrapersonal and interpersonal knowing (self-knowledge and "people skills"). He adds other ways of knowing to these original seven. Together the intelligences make a fuller picture of humanness and thus humanize classrooms.

Some Christian educators urge attention to progressive techniques. Christian day schools made use of progressive educator William Kilpatrick's (1871–1965) project method to mount science fairs and break out of routine. Church educator Marlene LeFever's championing of "learning styles" brought active learning to a whole generation of church education workers. Christian university education professors made use of "constructivist" approaches to prepare candidates to teach mathematics, literacy, science, and social studies. Education professor Harro Van Brummelen made a Christian reconstruction of learning styles and phases to help teachers develop meaningful learning experiences. Curriculum publishers programmed many more crafts and projects into early-years education for churches. Youth curriculum included discussion breakouts. Seminaries remained mostly untouched, focused on the traditional academic rigor needed for subjects of a "theological encyclopedia."[11] Overall, progressivism's impact on church-related education has been modest.[12]

RECONSTRUCTION

Christian educators should question progressivism. Is discovery learning faithful to revealed Christian beliefs? Broadly, how should conservative Christians understand John Dewey, Howard Gardner, or Paulo Freire? At points, their approaches challenge orthodox Christian beliefs.

---

[11] Edward Farley, "Four Pedagogical Mistakes: A Mea Culpa," *Teaching Theology & Religion* 8, no. 4 (October 2005): 200–3.
[12] Harro W. Van Brummelen, *Walking with God in the Classroom* (Colorado Springs: Purposeful Design Publications, 2009), 122–25.

At the same time, constructivism raises questions for Christian educators that they should not ignore. Do pupils construct more accurate or less accurate understandings of their world? Piaget's career was launched when he realized what variation in student answers to a test of intelligence meant. He noticed that wrong answers from a given age group were wrong in predictable ways. Students construct wrongly when they lack capacities for conceptualization that develop later, as their schooling continues. In the later stages, students demonstrated learning that was closer to physical reality. Piaget went on to posit key transition points in learning capacities. Are constructivists right that identifying student interest made genuine teaching possible? Techniques based on learning theories that address the subject-object split hold some promise.

To address the subject-object split, the innovative philosopher of science Michael Polanyi developed a whole-person approach to scientific knowledge. Education thinkers including Parker Palmer use Polanyi to mix subjectivist and empirical real-world approaches to teaching. Since learning centers around a real subject, they believe that the external world is knowable, but also recognize the subjectivist insight that pupils construct knowledge. They argue that human beings always understand reality by a system of rules. The rules together amount to a paradigm, a way of seeing. As students learn to speak a language, they gain the ability to name important features of the world. Empiricism, broadly, says the opposite: the facts add up to a theory; a paradigm comes after the facts are in. In the empiricist approach, the scientist conducts experiments; after a time, data can be reasoned into a whole theory. The contrasting paradigm, or "rules first" insight, meant that a way of seeing—a theory—pointed out empirical facts that mattered while bypassing other facts.[13]

In the "rules first" way of seeing, the governing paradigm is the Bible as understood by a particular tradition. The Bible's narrative

[13] Michael Polanyi, *Personal Knowledge: Towards a Post-Critical Philosophy* (Chicago: University of Chicago Press, 1958); Polanyi, *The Tacit Dimension* (Chicago: University of Chicago Press, 2009).

leads to a way of seeing the world. The Bible is the framework for understanding—a "plausibility structure."

Another approach to the subject-object split was developed by narrative thinkers. These thinkers see the key to education, and psychology and other fields, in the fact that human beings make sense of themselves and their world by using stories. Canadian educator Kieran Egan's narrative imaginative learning may enable Christians to use constructivist techniques with faithful integrity.[14]

SUMMARY OF PROGRESSIVE EDUCATION

Progressivism lived out its world through its Memory, Vision, Symbols, and Ethos:

- Progressivism's **Memory** defied the Scientific Revolution's split of the human subject from objective knowledge. John Locke's best-known challenger, Rousseau, was arguably the founder of the tradition.
- Progressivism's **Vision** was universal liberty, equality, and fraternity (the slogan of the French Revolution); it worked to implement its Vision of eliminating causes of human alienation as it understood them.
- **Symbols** and rituals included inclusive practices enshrined in law.
- Its **Ethos** reflects an optimism about human potentials that denied or re-labeled stubborn human perversity.

Christians need a theory that is faithful to revelation that allows for more than one best scientific way to teach. Progressivism's learning theory, *constructivism*, recognizes the variable learning processes of pupils. Apologetic efforts of Christian theorists rendered some progressive educational approaches as consistent with Christian beliefs—pointers to the way forward. Being faithful both to the hard reality of the world and to the personal ways of understanding it could open a new era of Christian education research.

---

[14] Parker J. Palmer, *The Courage to Teach: Exploring the Inner Landscape of a Teacher's Life*, 1st ed. (San Francisco: Jossey-Bass, 1997); Kieran Egan, *The Educated Mind: How Cognitive Tools Shape Our Understanding* (Chicago: University of Chicago Press, 1997).

7

THE NEXT CHRISTIAN EDUCATION

The Scientific Revolution changed Christian culture. Four centuries later, the empirical way of thinking penetrates every area of modern society with only a few exceptions. Powerful and subtle expectations influence all schools and universities. Scholars vindicate their scholarship in public scholarly organizations, and Christian scholars are not exceptions. Christian scholars in science, social sciences, or the humanities—any non-theological discipline—must make a public case based on authorities that are publicly acceptable. In a culture that prizes scientific knowledge, scholars must place brackets around knowledge that comes from revelation. Business-style rationalization seems so natural that Christian schools, churches, seminaries, and universities adopt sharp-edged tools of efficiency. Cultural habits are hard to break. Modern ideas of "success" are deeply embedded.

Follow this thought experiment about how faith is treated in modern settings: a colleague at work converts to Buddhism and begins to practice his new faith at a meditation center on weekends. Perhaps his step responds to the busyness, pressures, and high level of organization that rationalized life demands. His religion is not a public but a private matter. His religion is his option. The new practice is not likely to affect him during the week. Colleagues, friends, and relatives may remain unaware of his new commitment. The point? Scientific knowledge and practices are publicly acceptable, but religious knowledge is private—an option for persons and subcultures that choose it.

CHRISTIAN EDUCATION IN A SCIENTIFIC CULTURE

To trace the influence of present-day scientific culture on Christian education, let's look at four cases. I placed them together, so you can notice the similarity of cultural pressures on Christian schools, seminaries, colleges, and families.

Case One. An association of Christian schools trumpets its "success." Its graduates are "outstanding" by secular measures of ability in mathematics and literacy. Enrollment rises as Christian parents respond to and pay for "success," defined by the educational measurements of the wider culture. Questions are left open: Is the Christian school succeeding at specifically Christian education? Will its graduates bear witness to Christ in their vocations?

John Hull, a Christian professor of education, shows how scientific education's subtle persistence shapes Christian education in late modern cultures. Imagine concentric circles of specifically *Christian* influences on day-school students. The narrowest circle is when the school simply models Christian attitudes toward learning. In the next circle, the schools influence students in Christian ethical directions. In the third circle, the school presents foundational perspectives. The fullest circle leads students into worldview perspectives. Hull says that Christian day schools generally go no further than the first circle, modeling Christian attitudes toward learning. The reason for the weak showing, he says, is that "real schooling" in modern Western settings must conform to the dominant empiricism.

Empirical education continually defies modifications. It persistently reverts to managing and measuring. Twentieth-century movements of progressive curriculum reformers struggled and failed to modify public schooling. The empirical education that resisted progressive reformers also resists Christian efforts to reform the public-school model. Imagining alternative schools that lead to mainstream participation in jobs or social recognition is difficult.

The Christian school movement was founded to counter the displacement of Christian beliefs from classrooms. Founders wanted to give credit to Christian beliefs. Christian schools write strong statements of intent that promise graduates who will live out a Christian worldview. Yet, redefining secular knowledge to line up with Christian belief is difficult in a society where "success" has a secular definition. The public-school model of education is so well established that its practices are what "school" looks like. For anyone brought up in a modern society, the empirical schooling model stretches across the horizon like a harvest moon. A rival tradition is not just set out on paper and in speeches. It must be embodied and enacted. The Christian school movement's strong statements remain aspirations.[1]

Whether countercultural lives develop from schooling depends not only on an intellectual statement of intent. It depends also on the ecology of church, family, and mass media; on the structures and disciplines of the hidden curriculum. It is the power of an ecology of Memory, Vision, Symbols, and Ethos that makes a lived-worldview approach so insightful.

Intellectual statements do not necessarily add up to successful Christian education. For example, a philosophy of education derived from Thomas Aquinas (1225–1274) sometimes underpins the current movement of classical schools. The explicit rationale could give schools an educational coherence.[2] However, success requires that the philosophy of education be worked into the many specific practices of disciplined learning. Teachers and students who want the rationale to succeed must commit themselves to doing

---

[1] Gloria G. Stronks and Doug Blomberg, eds., *A Vision with a Task: Christian Schooling for Responsive Discipleship* (Grand Rapids, MI: Baker, 1993), 23–25, 32.

[2] P. D. Spears and S. R. Loomis, *Education for Human Flourishing: A Christian Perspective* (Downers Grove, IL: IVP Academic, 2009).

education in unconventional ways, and to do so will require persistent social supports.[3]

To reclaim the Christian intellectual tradition of education, setting out one more philosophical statement is not enough. Wilfred Carr, a British philosopher of education, boldly asks why academic philosophy of education rarely affects the decisions of education systems. He concludes that practical and political considerations drive decision-making in most education. His solution is a philosophy of education that understands education dynamically—practically, that is, as part of a living tradition.

> Previous generations of practitioners (reinterpreted their work) in order to find answers to the kind of practical questions that they had to face—questions which they could only resolve by reflectively revising and reconstructing the pre-reflective understanding of their practice that tradition had provided to them.[4]

Influencing students toward a lived Christian worldview requires a Christian educational paradigm. Carr's call for a practical philosophy of education is a call to Christian educators also. Effective Christian education demands that designers must revise and reconstruct a new education. They must challenge inherited ways of thinking about education.

Hull calls educators to "paradigm warfare." Only a revolution in education thinking can foster worldview-level Christian day schooling. Teachers and administrators must connect "teaching, curriculum planning, student evaluations, goal selection, and . . . the way we structure the school situation" with Christian "transforming, healing, cleansing, sorting, correcting, affirming, deepening, focusing, separating, and prioritizing." He cautions,

---

[3] J. E. Hull, "Aiming for Christian Education, Settling for Christians Educating: The Christian School's Replication of a Public School Paradigm," *Christian Scholars Review* 32, no. 2 (2003): 217–22; Stronks and Blomberg, *A Vision with a Task*.

[4] Wilfred Carr, "Philosophy and Education," *Journal of Philosophy of Education* 38, no. 1 (2004): 55–73.

> If we cannot describe faithful education in these concrete terms, the Christian perspective will continue to perform like book-ends—God talk will appear at the beginning and end of lessons, units, courses and school years, but what lies in between will remain largely unaffected.

Christian day schoolers aim for Christian education, he says, but settle for Christians educating.[5]

Case Two. In the US and Canada, roughly one hundred schools affiliate with the Council of Christian Colleges and Universities, plus another two hundred institutions that form the Association for Biblical Higher Education. The evangelical college and university movement in North America developed from Bible colleges founded by conservative Protestant denominations or independent groups. The oldest American universities including Harvard, Yale, and Columbia, along with more recent ones such as Johns Hopkins, Chicago, or Stanford, accepted scientific claims about human origins in the late 1800s and accepted historical and literary claims that viewed the Bible as any other book. In the 1920s and 1930s, Protestant churches divided over such claims. Efforts in the 1950s and 1960s to re-insert conservative European theology of the day as a new Christian basis of university education failed.[6]

The evangelical university movement contradicted mainstream education's secularization. It questioned scientific approaches that presented themselves as neutral and objective. The mission of most evangelical colleges was an integration of Christian beliefs and secular knowledge. Evangelical higher education sought to recast scholarly disciplines to conform them to classic Christian beliefs. It proposed to transform mainstream knowledge by asserting that the triune God is the universal Creator. Logically, no "secular" domain exists outside God's control, authority, and presence. In effect, it

---

[5] Hull, "Aiming for Christian Education," 222–23.
[6] Douglas Sloan, *Faith and Knowledge: Mainline Protestantism and American Higher Education* (Louisville, KY: Westminster John Knox Press, 1994).

aimed to re-sacralize the secular by bringing knowledge captive to Christ (2 Cor. 10:5).

Today, many evangelical universities offer pre-service teacher education as well as post-graduate education. Their education departments prepare teachers for evangelical day schools and public schools. Usually the future teachers do identical course-work. Christians who prepare teachers for public settings thus engage in a juggling act. Expression of Christian beliefs is taboo in most public schools. Yet their candidates must have public-school competencies and be willing to function as members of a public-school staff. Disrupters of the status quo would not be employed for long. Teacher preparation focuses on processes or structures of learning in literacy, mathematics, or social stud-ies instruction. However, the cultural dominance of the scientific model reduces the need that future teachers feel for a specifically Christian integration. Education professors, aware that empiri-cal education pushes faith to the margins, reconcile Christian beliefs with public (and Christian) school practices. They sift mainstream theories for conformity to Christian beliefs, which serve as "control beliefs." Examples include writings on Christian beliefs for inclusion, classroom management, learning theories, or language learning approaches.[7]

Case Three. Education for ministers in seminaries fits into the research university model. After the 1800s, theology adopted a sci-entific approach. The curriculum of scientifically influenced theol-ogy became an "encyclopedia" of abstract theological subjects. The result was that theory disconnected from practice. Connecting the practice of ministry with abstractions remains difficult.

---

[7] Matthew Etherington, *What Teachers Need to Know: Topics in Diversity and Inclusion* (Eugene, OR: Wipf and Stock, 2017); David I. Smith and Susan M. Felch, *Teaching and Christian Imagination* (Grand Rapids, MI: Eerdmans, 2015); David I. Smith and James K. A. Smith, *Teaching and Christian Practices: Reshaping Faith and Learning* (Grand Rapids, MI: Eerdmans, 2011); David I. Smith and Barbara Maria Carvill, *The Gift of the Stranger: Faith, Hospitality, and Foreign Language Learn-ing* (Grand Rapids, MI: Eerdmans, 2000); Nicholas Wolterstorff, Gloria G. Stronks, and Clarence Joldersma, *Educating for Life: Reflections on Christian Teaching and Learning* (Grand Rapids, MI: Baker Academic, 2002).

Theological seminaries to train pastors developed historically as counterpart to the research university. As with day schools, the scientific model remains the model with cultural authority. Theologian-historians Edward Farley, David Kelsey, and others propose holistic, practical models of theological education. Theology needs to be public (not private) truth, and the box in which science placed religion needs to be broken open.

Case Four. Protestant church educators call church leaders to remedy members' limited understanding of Christian teachings. Farley laments,

> Why is it that the vast majority of Christian believers remain largely unexposed to Christian learning—to historical-critical studies of the Bible, to the content and structure of the great doctrines, to two thousand years of classic works on the Christian life, to basic disciplines of theology, biblical languages, Christian ethics? Why do bankers, lawyers, farmers, physicians, homemakers, scientists, salespeople, managers of all sorts, people who carry out all kinds of complicated tasks in their work and home, remain at a literalist, elementary school level in their religious understanding? How is it that high school age church members move easily and quickly into the complex world of computers, foreign languages, DNA, and calculus, and cannot even make a beginning in historical-critical interpretation of a single text of Scripture?[8]

Some educators want to restart systematic instruction, similar to the catechesis of the Hellenistic Christian education. Proposers of systematic instruction assert that the reasonable aim of church education is whole-person worship of the Triune God. Church education of human beings should be oriented exactly toward the aim. An effective instruction plan should systematically present topic after topic. The calendar of the traditional church worship makes for natural occasions for Christian teaching—Advent, Christmas,

---

[8] Edward Farley, "Can Church Education Be Theological Education?," *Theology Today* 42, no. 2 (July 1985), 165.

Easter, Pentecost, Ascension Day, etc. The church calendar thus can shape individual lives. Farley supports a revival of systematic church teaching. He deals with the congregational ignorance problem by adding a curriculum writer and staff teacher. They will teach theology at various student levels. He basically opts for a straightforward reassertion of the church's teaching role.[9]

Renewing systematic church education by "just doing it" like these restarters seems to have history's support. The earliest practice of churches was methodical teaching of a creed wrapped in membership of a catechumenate, marked by distinct rituals of initiation. Enacted and embodied rituals were themselves part of the education. Proposals for simply renewing systematic teaching assume a firm division of sacred from secular, both in time and in educational theory.

Nobody will disagree that local churches should teach Scripture and doctrine. But local church sociology is apt to block the ideal. Current patterns of doing church are historical habits with deep roots, as Farley and Yale church education professor Dwayne Huebner showed. The modern educational ecology is a different one than the ancient countercultural ecology of churches, families, and peers that we saw in Hellenistic Christian education. Many factors work together to pass on a culture to a new generation. Educational traditions are set by cultural paradigms, as this guide shows. Reasserting topic-by-topic teaching looks like a solution—until one appreciates education has an ecology. Reformers need to consider the whole context.[10]

These four cases show different kinds of Christian education responding to empiricism's narrow box. School, university, church, and family respond differently to the intellectual and social context

[9] Debra Dean Murphy, *Teaching That Transforms: Worship as the Heart of Christian Education* (Eugene, OR: Wipf and Stock, 2007), 18–21; Gary Parrett and J. I. Packer, *Grounded in the Gospel: Building Believers the Old-Fashioned Way* (Grand Rapids, MI: Baker, 2010).

[10] Michael Warren, "Religious Formation in the Context of Social Formation," in *Critical Perspectives on Christian Education: A Reader on the Aims, Principles and Philosophy of Christian Education*, ed. Jeff Astley and Leslie J. Francis (Leominster, UK: Gracewing, 1994).

of empiricism, but they also find themselves reshaped in scientific culture. The four cases point to ways to reclaim a specifically Christian tradition of education.

RECLAIMING FAMILY EDUCATION

Christian families are key to propagating Christian faith. Christian marriage, according to classical scholar Sarah Ruden, was "as different from anything before or since as the command to turn the other cheek." In a culture that made slaves into sex objects—especially women and boys—Jesus's insistence on chastity came as relief. The meaning of sex changed. What one does with sex was no longer separated from one's character. The Christian revolution in fourth-century Rome introduced a radical sexual discipline that created the Christian family.[11]

The releasing of cultural sanctions on sex outside of marriage after the 1960s indicates nothing less than that the Christian worldview lost its hold. Urbanization and changed work patterns augmented the shift away from the family. At the everyday level, divorce—or both parents working—could mean that a child did not get to church regularly. Statistically, the decline of the family contributes to decline of religious practice. Christian families and Christian beliefs arguably make a "double helix" of faith propagation. Both strands of DNA are essential for reproduction.[12]

---

[11] Sarah Ruden, *Paul Among the People: The Apostle Reinterpreted and Reimagined in His Own Time* (New York: Image Books, 2010), 102; Kyle Harper, *From Shame to Sin: The Christian Transformation of Sexual Morality in Late Antiquity* (Cambridge, MA: Harvard University Press, 2013); Rod Dreher, "Sex After Christianity," *The American Conservative* 12, no. 2 (April 2013): 20–23; The pioneering work on the Christian cultural revolution is Peter R. L. Brown, *The Body and Society: Men, Women, and Sexual Renunciation in Early Christianity* (New York: Columbia University Press, 1988).

[12] Philip Rieff, *The Triumph of the Therapeutic: Uses of Faith After Freud* (Chicago: University of Chicago Press, 1987), 62; "Exodus: Why Americans Are Leaving Religion—and Why They're Unlikely to Come Back," *PRRI* (blog), accessed October 2, 2016, http://www.prri.org/research/prri-rns–2016-religiously-unaffiliated-americans/; Julie Zauzmer, "How Decades of Divorce Helped Erode Religion," *Washington Post*, September 27, 2016, sec. Acts of Faith, https://www.washingtonpost.com/news/acts-of-faith/wp/2016/09/27/how-decades-of-divorce-helped-erode-religion/; Elizabeth Marquardt, Charles E. Stokes, and Amy Zeittlow, "Does the Shape of Families Shape Faith?: Challenging the Churches to Confront the Impact of Family Change," in *Torn Asunder: Children, the Myth of the Good Divorce, and the Recovery of Origins*, ed. Margaret McCarthy (Grand Rap-

Parental faith largely correlates with their children's faith. Two believing parents who practice their faith stand nearly a fifty-fifty chance of passing on their faith: "Where both parents belong to the same denomination, the proportion of children maintaining that allegiance and the proportion listing themselves as 'none' are equal at 46 percent each." However, if only one parent is religious—usually the mother—around 22 percent of children will follow suit. Non-allegiance to religion is almost always passed on: when neither parent is religiously affiliated, 91 percent of their grown children say they have no religion. Each successive age cohort in Britain and Europe in the past 150 years shows lowered belief and lower practice compared to its predecessor. The United States is not an exception to these trends, as a series of articles by David Voas and collaborators shows. At individual and family levels, the "secularization" process is better named "dechristianization." Taking a global perspective on the statistics, Voas's future looks bleak. Families are central and irreplaceable in propagating the faith.[13]

Small patterns of hope that continue to grow become significant, however. We can also analyze change at the margins, as economists do. Researcher Vern Bengtson traced families over four decades. His data indicates that families remain important in faith formation. Six in ten of his sample had the same religious affiliation as their parents. Four in ten had the same affiliation as their grandparents, and similar levels of intensity, participation, biblical literalism, and civic religiosity. For evangelicals, fathers were especially important. A child who is emotionally close to his father is

---

ids, MI: Eerdmans, 2017), 66–90; Mary Eberstadt, *How the West Really Lost God: A New Theory of Secularization* (West Conshohocken, PA: Templeton Press, 2013).

[13] David Voas, "The Rise and Fall of Fuzzy Fidelity in Europe," *European Sociological Review* 25, no. 2 (2009): 155–68; David Voas and Mark Chaves, "Is the United States a Counterexample to the Secularization Thesis?," *American Journal of Sociology* 121, no. 5 (March 2016): 1517–56; David Voas and Alasdair Crockett, "Religion in Britain: Neither Believing nor Belonging," *Sociology* 39, no. 1 (February 2005): 11–28; David Voas and Stefanie Doebler, "Secularization in Europe: Religious Change Between and Within Birth Cohorts," *Religion and Society in Central and Eastern Europe* 4, no. 1 (2011): 39–62.

25 percent more likely to claim the same faith. Mothers, perhaps always more likely to be close to a child, account for only a single point of difference.[14]

Protestant churches can design education to support their families. They can dramatize life transitions through deliberate markers. Christ himself undeniably instituted central Christian rituals of baptism and communion. In these rituals, bodily participation matches mental assent. Rituals make church adherence public, like a wedding ceremony makes a marriage public. We noted earlier how the early church moved adherents into full membership by a series of rituals that marked their steps of initiation. Formal ceremonies characterize many institutions, including democratic institutions with the ritual of voting. Boy Scouts founder Robert Baden-Powell adapted ceremonies and structures for his movement as it formed in 1907. Churches in the Reformation heritage are suspicious of rituals. Lutherans and later Protestants criticized Catholics for "empty ritual." However, along with relationships, rhetoric, and roles, rituals can be important to young-adult conversion. Recent books outline pathways into adulthood, with titles such as *Raising a Modern-Day Knight*, *The Young Man in the Mirror: A Rite of Passage into Manhood*, and *Young Lions: Christian Rites of Passage for African-American Young Men*.[15]

---

[14] Vern L. Bengtson, Norella M. Putney, and Susan Harris, *Families and Faith: How Religion Is Passed Down across Generations* (New York: Oxford University Press, 2013); Naomi Schaefer Riley, "From Generation to Generation," *Wall Street Journal - Eastern Edition* 263, no. 21 (January 27, 2014): A11; Amy Frykholm, "Families of Faith," *Christian Century*, December 25, 2013; Susanna M. Steeg, "Families and Faith: How Religion Is Passed Down across Generations," *International Journal of Christianity & Education* 19, no. 1 (March 1, 2015): 77–78.

[15] Charles R. Foster, *From Generation to Generation: The Adaptive Challenge of Mainline Protestant Education in Forming Faith* (Eugene, OR: Cascade Books, 2012); Maxwell E. Johnson, *The Rites of Christian Initiation: Their Evolution and Interpretation* (Collegeville, MN: Liturgical Press, 2007), 212; David P. Setran and Chris A. Kiesling, *Spiritual Formation in Emerging Adulthood: A Practical Theology for College and Young Adult Ministry* (Grand Rapids, MI: Baker Academic, 2013); Robert Lewis, *Raising a Modern-Day Knight: A Father's Role in Guiding His Son to Authentic Manhood* (Carol Stream, IL: Tyndale, 2007); Patrick Morley, *The Young Man in the Mirror: A Rite of Passage into Manhood* (Nashville, TN: B&H, 2003); Chris McNair, *Young Lions: Christian Rites of Passage for African-American Young Men* (Nashville, TN: Abingdon Press, 2001).

To reclaim the Christian tradition of education, family support and encouragement should become a key local-church ministry. An organization such as Ron Hunter's "D6" can provide continuity of Vision that denominations have largely let fall.

RECLAIMING CHRISTIAN SCHOOLING AND UNIVERSITIES

Cloistered settings formed whole lives for worship. Cloisters were Christian worship, life, and education in refined form. They developed Christian schooling in their elementary and advanced forms. Where classical tutoring did not include a son's character, the all-in-one character of monastery and cathedral education emphasized the moral dimension. All subjects were taught from the Christian point of view—an aspect of a faith that seeks to inform all of life (Col. 2:6–15). The founding sociologist Emile Durkheim and education historian Henri Marrou suggest that Western education's moral intensity stems from its earliest setting in the cloister. More recent consideration of the AD 300s Christian revolution suggests that personal-desire management also went with the cloistered form of schooling. Boys and girls attended separate schools, after all. While schooling for males and females was conditioned by cultural norms for their future work, the absence of females from monasteries (and males from convents) clearly had something to do with desire management. Along with vows of poverty and obedience, chastity was the foundational vow of a monk. Schools and universities grew from these intensive forms of social life.

Understanding education as worship implies closer ties in the educational ecology. Family, church, and school must together forge the community of faith. If schools and universities are to tell the Christian cultural story well, they must imagine themselves as community centers. There the cultural story is lived out and exhibited, applauded, celebrated, and encouraged. A community center will be a site of artistic expression, public extensions of knowledge and reflection, and family life.

Schools and universities should reimagine their work as Christian cultural centers. Some Christian universities integrate their efforts around the conception of a lived Christian worldview. Recent proposals for university life put whole-life worship at the center. Worship of the triune God serves as a centering concept for the whole person, body, mind, and spirit. Is it an accident that the birth of Christian schooling came from a place where life revolved around worship? The desire for fuller worship led naturally to study and schooling. Christian schools and universities must resume the work of cultural storytelling.[16]

A unified conception of knowledge is a unique benefit of a Christian university or school. Empirical education fragments knowledge, as we saw previously. Christian schools retain the basis for a unified education—a unified view of reality drawn from the knowledge that God created everything. Naturally, Christian knowledge is not exhaustive. Finite beings lack a God's-eye view. That lack humbles a believer and opens him to hear from those with whom he disagrees. Nevertheless, the unitary conception of truth that fueled Christian education from its monastic birthplace still gives an unmatched basis for a confident education in liberal arts and sciences. In the age of the "multiversity," Christian colleges are potentially among the only holistic educators left. Confidence in God brings a responsibility to lecturing or seminar leadership, to mentoring and assessing, which pragmatic education often lacks.[17]

RECLAIMING CHURCH EDUCATION

For decades, evangelical, Anglican, and Catholic writers have noticed a strange loss of urgency about Christian education. Their book titles include *Will There Be Faith?*, *Is It a Lost Cause?*, and

[16] James K. A. Smith, *Desiring the Kingdom: Worship, Worldview, and Cultural Formation*, Cultural Liturgies (Grand Rapids, MI: Baker Academic, 2009); Murphy, *Teaching That Transforms*.
[17] Brian J. Walsh, "Transformation: Dynamic Worldview or Repressive Ideology?," *Journal of Education and Christian Belief* 4, no. 2 (2000): 101–14; R. W. Jenson, "On the Renewing of the Mind," in *Essays in Theology of Culture* (Grand Rapids, MI: Eerdmans, 1995), 163–74.

Will Our Children Have Faith? Church educator Charles Foster's *From Generation to Generation* has a subtitle about an adaptive challenge to mainline Protestant education. An "adaptive challenge" is one where existing knowledge and know-how will not suffice. Foster charges that "denominations encountered cultural challenges to their identities and missions in the decades after World War II (and) largely abandoned commitments to education as a means to envision a lively and robust future for themselves through their children and youth." Now, "changing values, behaviors, and attitudes" indicate "experiments, new discoveries, and adjustments." Given young-adult adherence statistics, conservative Protestants cannot exempt themselves from the generational challenge. Thinkers such as Richard Osmer and Friedrich Schweitzer lament religious education's loss of audience. "Loss of audience" for faith education understates something very wrong.[18]

Jesus taught the earliest church—the inner circle of disciples—to be cultural storytellers. He taught disciples to thrust meaningful gestures into the public square. Disciples with only a private knowledge that the promises and history of Israel culminated in Jesus of Nazareth, the promised Messiah, Savior, and pioneer of a new world order, were never likely to propagate the movement. When Jesus healed on the Sabbath, when he touched untouchables, when he forgave sins, when he identified himself as the genuine Bread of Life, when he justified himself by stories and sayings that subverted the status quo—he embodied his own story. Jesus publicly modeled meaning-laden action in the world so that his inner circle took up his cultural storytelling—care for the dying, feeding the hungry, engaging in mission, teaching the Word. Public storytell-

---

[18] Thomas H. Groome, *Will There Be Faith?: A New Vision for Educating and Growing Disciples* (New York: HarperOne, 2011); Marva J. Dawn, *Is It a Lost Cause?: Having the Heart of God for the Church's Children* (Grand Rapids, MI: Eerdmans, 1997); John H. Westerhoff, *Will Our Children Have Faith?*, rev. ed (Harrisburg, PA: Morehouse, 2000); Foster, *From Generation to Generation*, 5, 8; R. R. Osmer and F. Schweitzer, *Religious Education Between Modernization and Globalization: New Perspectives on the United States and Germany* (Grand Rapids, MI: Eerdmans, 2003).

ing requires an institutionalized form that Jesus himself appears to have anticipated (Matt. 18:15–35).[19]

Church as a cultural storyteller continues to the present. Local church as an enacted witness means that participation by members must include learning some version of the story. Churches can tell the story poorly or well. Members who absorb their (wide sense) education will either discredit or bring credit to the story. Meaningful actions and disciplined learning educate. Church itself is education.

The church needs to reclaim the story in order to tell it. The question, "What is the gospel?" can focus efforts, as does Bonhoeffer's question, "Who is Jesus Christ for us today?" Church practices teach Christ as understood in that time and place. *Missio dei*—the mission of God—is a way of speaking of church as God's love in sending Christ and the church to the world. Churches can regroup under the banner of mission. The renewed story brings renewed church identity and mission.[20]

Recognizing how pervasive cultural storytelling is can lead away from theoretical ideas of church life into a story-formed or narrative way of practical theology. Rituals tell cultural stories as meaningful gestures. Recognizing storytelling in actions means that as written or oral texts tell stories, performances tell stories too. Performances make unwritten "texts." So "rhetorical practical theology" understands church life as a kind of persuasive speech—a cultural storytelling process. The gospel is "rhetorically" expressed in what churches do. The gospel is also contradicted in what churches do not do. From this perspective, a spoken-and-lived story of mission forms a frame for all church-sponsored, disciplined learning.

---

[19] Ted Newell, "Worldviews in Collision: Jesus as Critical Educator," *Journal of Education & Christian Belief* 13, no. 2 (2009): 141–54.

[20] Richard R. Osmer, "Practical Theology: A Current International Perspective," *HTS Teologiese Studies / Theological Studies* 67, no. 2 (November 16, 2011): 5; Stuart Murray, *Church Planting: Laying Foundations* (Scottdale, PA: Herald Press, 2001); Lesslie Newbigin, *The Gospel in a Pluralist Society* (Grand Rapids, MI: Eerdmans, 1989).

"Church as mission" gives leaders a wider context and thus wider conception of disciplined learning. Programs such as grief recovery, divorce care, or the Alpha movement's catechetical evangelism express the gospel with head and hands. Christian schooling, whether church sponsored or by the loose church of an independent board, is concrete mission. Local churches' attention to members' growth in faith represent part of the mission of God. An example is Willow Creek's "Move" program. In each example, churches tell the master narrative against the mainstream culture's pervasive storytelling.[21]

Successive paradigms of Christian education in this guide underline for the reader that ordered learning operates in a historical context, within an ecology of family, church, and broader social supports. Education is a situated practice.

In 1951, the Yale theologian Richard Niebuhr produced a typology of theological stances to their host cultures, which has continued to provide a basic sorting scheme. For example, Niebuhr contrasted a separatist "Christ against culture" stance with a "Christ transforming culture" approach. "Christ above culture" characterized the Europe of cloistered education. The positions on the Niebuhr index will determine whether someone believes social-scientific findings to have merit. A "Christ against culture" thinker would refuse social-scientific findings; a "Christ transforming culture" thinker would use them when re-interpreted by Christian beliefs. It either leads to seeing the ongoing sexual revolution as moving toward biblical justice or as deepening the North American contradiction of the Bible. Differing Christian attitudes to a host culture are either keeping the nose of a camel out of a tent, or accessing valuable gold from Egyptians.[22]

---

[21] Tory K. Baucum, *Evangelical Hospitality: Catechetical Evangelism in the Early Church and Its Recovery for Today* (Lanham, MD: Scarecrow Press, 2008); Greg L. Hawkins and Cally Parkinson, *Move: What 1,000 Churches Reveal about Spiritual Growth* (Grand Rapids, MI: Zondervan, 2011).
[22] H. Richard Niebuhr, *Christ and Culture* (Harper & Row, 1975); D. A. Carson, *Christ and Culture Revisited* (Grand Rapids, MI: Eerdmans, 2008); Craig A. Carter, *Rethinking Christ and Culture: A Post-Christendom Perspective* (Grand Rapids, MI: Brazos Press, 2007); Bruce L. Guenther, "The

Churches wishing to resume responsibility as main nurturer of Christians must weigh the value of social-scientific findings. Use or non-use of sociology, anthropology, learning theory, and more seems like a technical issue until one considers that the choice implies practices. Rejection may mean relatively simple educational procedures. Roman Catholic catechists and religious educators argued about use of social sciences throughout the 1960s. Theologically minded catechists, focused on church membership and life, saw social-science findings as less important than theological categories. Religious educators, on the other hand, refused to see church practices as the highest expression of religiosity. They saw catechesis as questions and answers—the format that had repelled them as 1940s youths. The different attitudes toward secular disciplines generated strikingly different ways of educating.

The 1960s catechesis or religious education debate pivoted on the use of social sciences. The same issue still points to either doctrinal teaching or a broader conception of education. Both sides had points to commend their case. Both sides failed to transcend their categories. Church life as participation in the mission of God could be informed by any faithful knowledge.[23]

Churches that see their work as a fresh telling of the biblical story—in family ministry, in funerals, in personal visitation, in hospitality, in worship practices, in approaches to leadership, in committee work—have rich opportunities in a culture that is starving for hope.[24]

'Enduring Problem' of Christ and Culture," *Direction Journal*, accessed July 19, 2017, http://www
.directionjournal.org/34/2/enduring-problem-of-christ-and-culture.html; Austin Harrington, "Social
Theory and Theology," in *The Handbook of Contemporary European Social Theory*, ed. Gerard
Delanty (Abingdon, UK, and New York: Routledge, 2006), 37–47; John Milbank, *Theology and
Social Theory: Beyond Secular Reason*, 2nd ed. (Malden, MA; Oxford: Blackwell, 2006); Gregory
Baum, "Remarks of a Theologian in Dialogue with Sociology," in *Theology and the Social Sciences*,
ed. M. H. Barnes (Maryknoll, NY: Orbis Books, 2001), 3–11.

[23] Edward J. Newell, *"Education Has Nothing to Do with Theology": James Michael Lee's Social
Science Religious Instruction*, vol. 61, Princeton Theological Monograph series (Eugene, OR: Pickwick Publications, 2006).

[24] R. W. Jenson, "How the World Lost Its Story," *First Things* 36 (1993): 19–24.

SUMMARY OF THE NEXT CHRISTIAN EDUCATION

The guide started with the promise that renewed Christian education heralds and feeds Christian renewal. Its appearance is a sign of fresh confidence and growth. It named agents of renewal such as Charlemagne, Alcuin, the Protestant Reformers, John Wesley, and university founders. Of the paradigms, the earliest ecology of church and family looks most likely to nurture believers in the present-day pluralistic and postmodern setting. The earliest churches enacted hope for a worn-out culture and its many empty options. Christians' confidence in their story bred a tenacity that gained intellectual and political leadership of Rome in three centuries—from a handful of followers to an empire with many followers. The promise of Christian education remains rich. Education has no greater hope.

QUESTIONS FOR REFLECTION

CHAPTER 1: THE POTENTIAL OF CHRISTIAN EDUCATION

1. Which influences—parents, friends, siblings, mass media, sermons, youth group, sports, classrooms—would you see as most important to who you are now?

2. How did mass media influence your peer group and you?

3. Do written, null, and hidden curricula work together in your experience?

4. Why is disciplined or formal learning especially important for cultural minorities?

5. Why can Christian education be an agent for Christian renewal?

CHAPTER 2: JESUS'S EDUCATION

1. Think of a teacher who made a difference for you personally. Were the subject and the personal example totally disconnected?

2. How can students gain courage and vision to live counter to dominant culture?

3. Was Jesus more effective as a teacher before or after his death and resurrection?

4. Is education well defined as "passing on information"?

CHAPTER 3: CHRISTIAN EDUCATION IN HELLENISTIC CITY-STATES

1. How were *ekklesia* and *oikos* transformed by Christians?

2. Reflecting on chapter 3, why do you suppose the earliest Christians rarely if ever formed a separate enclave isolated from the wider culture?

3. Why were the earliest churches "in the world" but not "of the world"?

4. How important was education to the eventual Christian victory?

5. Why is contemporary Western popular culture little resisted by many present-day Christians?

6. What contribution could the pattern of Christian rituals have made to retaining young family members in the faith?

CHAPTER 4: CLOISTERED EDUCATION

1. Is it surprising, or only predictable, that universities developed by stages between 500 and 1200?

2. Why did abstract knowledge gradually take on more educational importance than the narratives of faith?

3. Does the early Christian concern for right desires and right thinking persist in present-day Western public education? Consider public schooling and mainstream universities.

4. Compared to Hellenistic Christian education, what was gained when the church gradually re-civilized Europe? What was lost?

5. Was European Christianity between 500 and 1200 unchanging or changing—static or dynamic?

CHAPTER 5: EMPIRICAL EDUCATION

1. Why is knowledge divided between empirical, scientific knowledge and human values?

2. Why did specifically Christian education become a minority church-related activity?

3. Which four factors gave rise to modern public schooling?

4. Why is education for specific religious beliefs difficult in public schools?

5. Does Bloom's taxonomy represent a distinct approach to teaching?

6. Is empirical education optimistic about original sin? Did it change curricula?

CHAPTER 6: PROGRESSIVE EDUCATION

1. Why is Rousseau an early—if not the first—progressivist?

2. How does progressivism react against empiricism?

3. The author mentions dedicated schools that implement the theory of a particular progressivist educator. When public schools use progressivist techniques, are they modifying empiricist practices? What was your own experience of progressivist learning in school?

4. Why does Dewey's theory raise issues for Christian thinkers?

CHAPTER 7: THE NEXT CHRISTIAN EDUCATION

1. Based on these reflections, what do you suggest for renewed Christian education in the twenty-first century?

TIMELINE

800 BC	• Homer (800 BC)
700 BC	• Hesiod (700 BC)
600 BC	
500 BC	• Greek Tragedians (500 BC–400 BC)
400 BC	• Plato (427–347 BC)
300 BC	• Aristotle (c. 384 BC–322 BC)
200 BC	
100 BC	
AD 0	• Jesus as teacher (AD 30–33) • Plutarch (AD 46–c. 125) • Paul (c. AD 6–c. 63) • Didache ("Teachings") (c. 96) • Clement of Rome (died c. 100)
AD 100	
AD 200	• Tertullian (c. 155–c. 240)
AD 300	
AD 400	• Augustine of Hippo (354–430) • John Cassian (c. 360–c. 435)
AD 500	• Pope Gregory the Great (540–604) • Columbanus's mission (585) • Augustine of Canterbury's mission (597)
AD 600	
AD 700	• Charlemagne (742–814) • Alcuin (c. 732–804)
AD 800	
AD 900	

AD 1000	
	• Pierre Abelard (1079–1142)
AD 1100	• Bonaventure (1221–1274) • Church-wide recognition of university degrees ("*ius ubique docendi*") (1289/1291)
AD 1200	• Martin Luther (1483–1546)
AD 1300	• First use of term "curriculum" (1582/1633) • J. A. Komensky ("Comenius") (1592–1670)
AD 1400	• John Locke (1632–1704) • J. J. Rousseau (1712–1778) • Rousseau's *Emile* (1762) • J. H. Pestalozzi (1746–1827) progressive Christian educator • Friedrich Froebel (1782–1852) progressive Christian educator • J. Bentham's utilitarian theory (1781)
AD 1500	
AD 1600	• Lancaster's "Improvements in Education" (1806) • American Sunday School Union (1824) • McGuffey's readers (1836) • Horace Mann becomes Sec. of Mass. Bd. of Education (1837) • Superintendent Philbrick's egg-crate school (1848) • Herbert Spencer's *Education: Intellectual, Moral, Physical* (1860) • U. S. hierarchy urges Catholic separate schools (1884)
AD 1700	
AD 1800	• John Dewey's *School and Society* (1900) • Founding of Religious Education Association (1903) • F. W. Taylor, efficiency expert (1856–1915) • Ford's Highland Park assembly line (1913) • F. Bobbitt's *How to Make a Curriculum* (1924)
AD 1900	• E. L. Thorndike, psychologist (1874–1949) disproved "transfer of learning" • B. Bloom's taxonomy (1956) • B. F. Skinner, behaviorist (1904–1990) • Jean Piaget's *Judgment and Reasoning in the Child* (1924, trans. 1928)—20th-century constructivism • Independent Christian Schooling 1960s • Homeschooling Movement 1970s
AD 2000	

GLOSSARY

Anthropology. The literal meaning is the "study of humanity." Knowledge about humanity can be posited from a theological standpoint, from a particular philosophy, or by collecting empirical data from the behaviors and speech of a group, among many approaches.

Classroom. An identified space for a group of students, developed in the modern era.

Curriculum. The basic meaning is a course or track that a teacher or school repeats at intervals, with predictable challenges. The term was rare in education in the ancient world. As the modern era developed predictable methods of education, it highlighted the term. Curriculum became a defined field of studies, launched by the book entitled *The Curriculum*, by Franklin Bobbitt (1918).

Ecology. A metaphorical way of conceiving the mutually supporting and reinforcing practices and beliefs that comprise a way of educating at a historical point in time. For example, the ecology of the modern era was fed by empiricism and expressed in efficient practices that used standardized methods to educate students for modern society.

Edification. A metaphorical extension of the building process, especially of a holy place such as a temple, to describe the work of developing the community life of a group such as a church.

Education. Literally, drawing out potentials latent in a person or group, thus, especially, a deliberate process of cultural development by emphasis on knowledge and aptitudes deemed important to the continued existence of a community. Only simple definitions avoid prejudice against other conceptions of education, so its most basic definition is "upbringing."

Empirical education. A way of teaching and learning that relies on evidence from the senses for its methods, based on a commitment to modern-era sciences.

Empiricism. The priority accorded to sense evidence over theoretical, speculative, or revealed knowledge.

Ethos. The way of being of a community, including their definitions of right and wrong, their morals, and their styles or preferences in beauty.

Gymnasiums. The educational and religious centers of Greek antiquity, including musical training and performances, athletics, and cult activities.

Hidden curriculum. The processes by which content is conveyed in a classroom or online space, resulting in specific characteristics in the students. Hidden curriculum includes methods of disciplining students whether based on morality or on pragmatic manipulation, teacher speech, routines and procedures that pass on conceptions of the relative worth of activities and persons, and the nature of the physical space and its location, among other factors.

Humanities. Primarily, linguistic and historical studies.

Koine Greek. The language spoken in the marketplace of the Hellenistic world, as distinct from the high language of philosophy or drama.

Memory. In this book, a technical term for the sense of history and tradition carried by a society or subculture that must be adopted and adapted by the rising generation. The term implies a flexible grasp of the past that alters over time, as an individual's memory alters over time.

Missio dei. Literally, the mission of God, a way of speaking of the Triune God's redemptive initiative in human history. The umbrella concept includes the Father's sending of his Son to save a people for himself, and also a church's tasks of evangelism and service for the building of God's kingdom.

Null curriculum. Content which is not taught, and by silence is evaluated as unimportant, shameful, or subversive of public order. Religion is possibly the most significant null curriculum in Western public schooling.

Paideia. Literally, the training of children. Metaphorically, a process of development and discipline toward an aim. It can be conceived broadly when the aim is enforced by political and legal power for political purposes.

Paradigm thinking. An approach that sees compatible beliefs as packages that comprise a way of thinking. Paradigm thinking does not take individual facts as recognizable unless a perceptual grid or filter makes them evident and visible. Worldview thinking and presuppositional apologetics are similar concepts.

Philosophy. Literally, the love of wisdom, or the pursuit by critical reflection of basic foundational understandings of a subject or of the world.

Progressive education. The form of education that developed as a reaction to scientific models that saw pupils as subjects for empirical manipulation; emphasizes that education must be meaningful to pupils, so, must be student-centered.

Progressivism. A movement with political and educational expressions that emphasises the historical liberation of human beings as they replace oppressive social structures with ongoing processes to maximize human freedom.

Psychology. The scientific study of human behavior.

Symbols. In this book, a technical term for the rituals and physical symbols that express the history and life of a community.

Utilitarianism. A philosophy of ethics developed first by the English thinker Jeremy Bentham (1748–1832) that assesses the worth of an activity by the relative amount of human happiness it produces.

Vision. In this book, a technical term for a society's sense of purpose and hope, the preferred future toward which it reaches.

RESOURCES FOR FURTHER STUDY

Ackroyd, Peter. *Foundation: The History of England from Its Earliest Beginnings to the Tudors*. New York: Thomas Dunne, 2011.

Adamson, J. W. "Education." In *The Legacy of the Middle Ages*, edited by C. G. Crump and E. F. Jacob, 255–85. Oxford: Clarendon Press, 1926.

Adelman, Clem. "Over Two Years, What Did Froebel Say to Pestalozzi?" *History of Education* 29, no. 2 (2000): 103–114.

———. "Play as a Quest for Vocation." *Journal of Curriculum Studies* 24, no. 2 (March 1, 1992): 139–51.

Agra Junker, Debora B. "Pestalozzi, Johann Heinrich." Edited by George T. Kurian and Mark A. Lamport. *Encyclopedia of Christian Education*. Lanham, Maryland: Rowman & Littlefield Publishers, 2015.

Alexander, Hanan A. "God as Teacher: Jewish Reflections on a Theology of Pedagogy." *Journal of Beliefs and Values* 22 (April 1, 2001): 5–17.

Alikin, Valeriy A. *The Earliest History of the Christian Gathering: Origin, Development and Content of the Christian Gathering in the First to Third Centuries*. Vol. 102. Supplements to Vigiliae Christianae. Leiden and Boston: Brill, 2010.

Allen, JoBeth. "Taylor-Made Education: The Influence of the Efficiency Movement on the Testing of Reading Skills." US Dept of Education Eric Document Reproduction Service No. ED 239 247, June 1984. ERIC.

Ando, C. "Augustine on Language." *Revue d'Etudes Augustiniennes et Patristiques* 40, no. 1 (January 1, 1994): 45–78.

Anyon, Jean. "Social Class and School Knowledge." *Curriculum Inquiry* 11, no. 1 (1981): 3–42.

Apple, Michael W. and Nancy R. King. "What Do Schools Teach?" *Curriculum Inquiry* 6, no. 4 (1977): 341.

Apple, Michael W. and Philip Wexler. "Cultural Capital and Educational Transmissions: An Essay on Basil Bernstein, Class, Codes and Control: Vol. III—Towards A Theory of Educational Transmissions." *Educational Theory* 28, no. 1 (1978): 34–43.

Arnold, Clinton E. "Early Church Catechesis and New Christians' Classes in Contemporary Evangelicalism." *Journal of the Evangelical Theological Society* 47, no. 1 (2004): 39–54.

Auerbach, Erich. *Mimesis: The Representation of Reality in Western Literature*. Translated by Willard R. Trask. Vol. 548. Princeton, NJ: Princeton University Press, 1953.

Axel, Gabriel. *Babette's Feast*. Irvington, NY: The Criterion Collection, 2013.

Azkoul, Michael. "The Greek Fathers: Polis and Paideia, Pt I." *St Vladimir's Theological Quarterly* 23, no. 1 (January 1, 1979): 3–21.

———. "The Greek Fathers: Polis and Paideia Pt II." *St Vladimir's Theological Quarterly* 23, no. 2 (January 1, 1979): 67–86.

Baker, Bernadette. "The Dangerous and the Good? Developmentalism, Progress, and Public Schooling." *American Educational Research Journal* 36, no. 4 (1999): 797–834.

Balch, David L. "Paul, Families, and Households." In *Paul in the Greco-Roman World: A Handbook*, edited by J. Paul Sampley, 1:198–227. Harrisburg, PA: Trinity Press International, 2003.

Bantock, G. H. *Artifice and Nature, 1350–1765*. Vol. 1. Studies in the History of Educational Theory. London: George Allen & Unwin, 1980.

Barr, James. *The Concept of Biblical Theology: An Old Testament Perspective*. Minneapolis, MN: Fortress Press, 2009.

Baucum, Tory K. *Evangelical Hospitality: Catechetical Evangelism in the Early Church and Its Recovery for Today*. Lanham, MD: Scarecrow Press, 2008.

Baum, Gregory. "Remarks of a Theologian in Dialogue with Sociology." In *Theology and the Social Sciences*. Edited by M. H. Barnes, 3–11. Maryknoll, NY: Orbis Books, 2001.

Bauman, Zygmunt. *Liquid Modernity*. Cambridge, UK, and Malden, MA: Polity Press, 2000.

———. *Liquid Times: Living in an Age of Uncertainty*. John Wiley & Sons, 2013.

Bayly, Joseph. "Evangelical Curriculum Development." *Religious Education* 75, no. 5 (1980): 539–45.

Bengtson, Vern L., Norella M. Putney, and Susan Harris. *Families and Faith: How Religion Is Passed Down across Generations*. New York: Oxford University Press, 2013.

Berman, Barbara. "Business Efficiency, American Schooling, and the Public School Superintendency: A Reconsideration of the Callahan Thesis." *History of Education Quarterly*, 1983: 297–321.

Bigg, Charles. *The Church's Task under the Roman Empire; Four Lectures with Preface, Notes, and an Excursus*. Oxford: Clarendon Press, 1905.

Blakley, J. Ted. "Incomprehension or Resistance?: The Markan Disciples and the Narrative Logic of Mark 4:1—8:30." University of St. Andrews, 2008.

Bloom, Benjamin S., ed. *Taxonomy of Educational Objectives: The Classification of Educational Goals, Handbook I: Cognitive Domain*. New York and London: Longman's, Green and Co., 1956.

Boran, Elizabethanne. "Ramus in Trinity College, Dublin in the Early Seventeenth Century." In *The Influence of Petrus Ramus: Studies in Sixteenth and Seventeenth Century Philosophy and Sciences*. Edited by M. Feingold, J. S. Freedman, and W. Rother, 177–99. Basel: Schwabe, 2001.

Bosch, David J. *Transforming Mission: Paradigm Shifts in Theology of Mission*. Vol. 16. American Society of Missiology Series. Maryknoll, NY: Orbis Books, 1991.

Boylan, Anne M. *Sunday School: The Formation of an American Institution, 1790–1880*. New Haven, CT: Yale University Press, 1990.

Boys, Mary C. *Educating in Faith: Maps and Visions*. New York: Harper & Row, 1989.

Brant, Jo-Ann A. "The Place of Mimēsis in Paul's Thought." *Studies in Religion/Sciences Religieuses* 22, no. 3 (1993): 285–300.

Brown, Lesley, and William R. Trumble, eds. "Science." *Shorter Oxford English Dictionary*. Oxford: Oxford University Press, 2002.

Brown, Peter. *The Rise of Western Christendom: Triumph and Diversity, A.D. 200–1000*. Chichester, UK and Malden, MA: Wiley-Blackwell, 2013.

Brown, Peter R. L. *The Body and Society: Men, Women, and Sexual Renunciation in Early Christianity*. New York: Columbia University Press, 1988.

Burbules, Nicholas C. "Tacit Teaching." *Educational Philosophy & Theory* 40, no. 5 (September 2008): 666–77.

Burge, Gary M., Lynn H. Cohick, and Gene L. Green. *The New Testament in Antiquity: A Survey of the New Testament within Its Cultural Context*. New York: Harper Collins, 2010.

Burkert, Walter. *Ancient Mystery Cults*. Cambridge: Harvard University Press, 1987.

Byrne, Catherine. *Religion in Secular Education: What, in Heaven's Name, Are We Teaching Our Children?* Vol. 21. International Studies in Religion and Society. Leiden: Brill, 2014.

Callahan, Raymond E. *Education and the Cult of Efficiency*. Chicago: University of Chicago Press, 1964.

Calvin, John. *Institutes of the Christian Religion*. Edited by John T. McNeill. Translated by Ford Lewis Battles. Vol. XX and XXI. Library of Christian Classics. Philadelphia, PA: Westminster Press, 1960.

Carey, Stephen. *A Beginner's Guide to Scientific Method*. Nelson Education, 2011.

Carr, Wilfred. "Philosophy and Education." *Journal of Philosophy of Education* 38, no. 1 (2004): 55–73.

Carson, D. A. *Christ and Culture Revisited*. Grand Rapids, MI: Eerdmans, 2008.

Carter, Craig A. *Rethinking Christ and Culture: A Post-Christendom Perspective*. Grand Rapids, MI: Brazos Press, 2007.

Cartwright, William H. "Education and the Cult of Efficiency: A Study of the Social Forces That Have Shaped the Administration of the Public Schools. By Raymond E. Callahan (Chicago: University of Chicago Press, 1962)." *Journal of American History* 49, no. 4 (March 1, 1963): 722–23.

Chin, Catherine. "Telling Boring Stories: Time, Narrative, and Pedagogy in De Catechizandis Rudibus." *Augustinian Studies* 37, no. 1 (January 2006): 43–62.

Cobban, Alan B. *The Medieval English Universities: Oxford and Cambridge to 1500*. Aldershot: Scholar Press, 1988.

Cochrane, Charles Norris. *Christianity and Classical Culture: A Study of Thought and Action from Augustus to Augustine*. Oxford: Oxford University Press, 1957.

Cohen, Shaye J. D. *From the Maccabees to the Mishnah*. 2nd ed. Louisville: Westminster John Knox Press, 2006.

"Comprehension: Bloom's Taxonomy." *Teacher's Corner, Omaha Public System* (blog). Accessed June 20, 2017. http://www.ops.org/reading/blooms_taxonomy.html via archive.org (first archived December 17, 1999).

Dawn, Marva J. *Is It a Lost Cause?: Having the Heart of God for the Church's Children*. Grand Rapids, MI: Eerdmans, 1997.

Dawson, Christopher. *Education and the Crisis of Christian Culture*. Chicago: Regnery, 1949.

De Zengotita, Thomas. *Mediated: How the Media Shapes Our World and the Way We Live in It*. New York: Bloomsbury Publishing USA, 2006.

———. "The Numbing of the American Mind: Culture as Anesthetic." *Harpers Magazine*, April 2002.

Deanesly, Margaret. *A History of the Medieval Church, 590–1500*. London: Methuen, 1925.

Décarreaux, Jean. *Monks and Civilization: From the Barbarian Invasions to the Reign of Charlemagne*. Translated by Charlotte Haldane. London: Allen & Unwin, 1964.

Denig, Stephen J. and Anthony J. Dosen. "The Mission of the Catholic School in the Pre-Vatican II Era (1810–1962) and the Post-Vatican II Era (1965–1995): Insights and Observations for the New Millennium." *Journal of Catholic Education* 13, no. 2 (2009): 2.

Denny, Frederick M., Margaret R. Miles, Charles Hallisey, and Earle H. Waugh. "Joachim Wach's 'Master and Disciple' Revisited: A Contemporary Symposium." *Teaching Theology & Religion* 1, no. 1 (February 1, 1998): 13–19.

Dericquebourg, Regis. "Religious Education in France." In *The Routledge International Handbook of Religious Education*. Edited by Derek Davis and Elena Miroshnikova, 113–21. Abingdon, UK and New York: Routledge, 2013.

Dickens, Charles. *Hard Times: For These Times*. London: Bradbury & Evans, 1854.

Dillon, J. T. "The Effectiveness of Jesus as a Teacher." *Lumen Vitae* 36, no. 2 (1981): 135–62.

———. *Jesus as a Teacher: A Multidisciplinary Case Study*. Bethesda, MD: International Scholars Publications, 1995.

Dreher, Rod. "Sex after Christianity." *The American Conservative* 12, no. 2 (April 2013): 20–23.

Durkheim, Emile. *The Evolution of Educational Thought: Lectures on the Formation and Development of Secondary Education in France*. Translated by P. Collins. London: Routledge & Kegan Paul, 1977.

Eberstadt, Mary. *How the West Really Lost God: A New Theory of Secularization*. West Conshohocken, PA: Templeton Press, 2013.

Egan, Kieran. *The Educated Mind: How Cognitive Tools Shape Our Understanding*. Chicago: University of Chicago Press, 1997.

———. "Students' Development in Theory and Practice: The Doubtful Role of Research." *Harvard Educational Review* 75, no. 1 (2005): 25–41.

———. *Primary Understanding: Education in Early Childhood*. London: Routledge, 1988.

Eisner, Elliot W. "Benjamin Bloom: 1913–1999." *Prospects* 30, no. 3 (2000): 387–95.

———. *The Educational Imagination: On the Design and Evaluation of School Programs*. 3rd edition. Upper Saddle River, NJ: Merrill Prentice Hall, 1994.

———. "Franklin Bobbitt and the 'Science' of Curriculum Making." *School Review* 75, no. 1 (Spring 1967): 29–47.

Elliott, Susan. "Mystery Cults." Edited by David Noel Freedman and Allen C. Myers. *Eerdmans Dictionary of the Bible*. Grand Rapids, MI: Eerdmans Publishing, 2000.

Etherington, Matthew. *What Teachers Need to Know: Topics in Diversity and Inclusion*. Eugene, OR: Wipf and Stock, 2017.

Evans, C. A. "What Did Jesus Do?" In *Jesus Under Fire: Modern Scholarship Reinvents the Historical Jesus*, 101–15. Grand Rapids, MI: Zondervan, 1995.

Evans, Craig A. *Fabricating Jesus: How Modern Scholars Distort the Gospels*. Downers Grove, IL: InterVarsity Press, 2006.

———. "The Jesus of History and the Christ of Faith: Toward Jewish-Christian Dialogue." In *Who Was Jesus? A Jewish-Christian Dialogue*. Edited by Paul Copan and C. A. Evans, 59–72, 174–78. Louisville, KY: Westminster/John Knox Press, 2001.

"Exodus: Why Americans Are Leaving Religion—and Why They're Unlikely to Come Back." *PRRI* (blog). Accessed October 2, 2016. http://www.prri.org/research /prri-rns–2016-religiously-unaffiliated-americans/.

Farley, Edward. "Can Church Education Be Theological Education?" *Theology Today* 42, no. 2 (July 1985): 158–71.

———. "Four Pedagogical Mistakes: A Mea Culpa." *Teaching Theology & Religion* 8, no. 4 (October 2005): 200–3.

———. "The Tragic Dilemma of Church Education." In *Caring for the Commonweal: Education for Religious and Public Life*, edited by Parker J. Palmer, Barbara G. Wheeler, and Robert W. Lynn, 131–45. Atlanta: Mercer University Press, 1990.

Fernhout, H. "Christian Schooling: Telling a World View Story." In *The Crumbling Walls of Certainty: Towards a Christian Critique of Postmodernity and Education*. Edited by I. Lambert and S. Mitchell, 75–96. Sydney: Centre for the Study of Australian Christianity, 1997.

Florovsky, Georges. "Empire and Desert: Antinomies of Christian History." *The Greek Orthodox Theological Review* 3, no. 2 (1957): 133–59.

Foster, Charles R. *From Generation to Generation: The Adaptive Challenge of Mainline Protestant Education in Forming Faith*. Eugene, OR: Cascade Books, 2012.

Francis, James. "Household." Edited by David Noel Freedman. *Eerdmans Dictionary of the Bible*. Grand Rapids, MI: Eerdmans, 2000.

Fraser, James W. *Between Church and State: Religion and Public Education in a Multicultural America*. 2nd ed. Baltimore, MD: JHU Press, 2016.

Frykholm, Amy. "Families of Faith." *Christian Century*, December 25, 2013.

Gauch, Hugh G. *Scientific Method in Practice*. Cambridge University Press, 2003.

Gerbner, G. *Against the Mainstream: The Selected Works of George Gerbner*. Edited by M. Morgan. New York: Peter Lang, 2002.

Gerbner, George. "Telling Stories in the Information Age." In *Information and Behavior*, edited by Brent D. Ruben, 3–12. New Brunswick, NJ and Oxford: Transaction Publishers, 1987.

Glasersfeld, Ernst von. "An Exposition of Constructivism: Why Some Like It Radical." In *Constructivist Views on the Teaching and Learning of Mathematics*, edited by Robert Davis, Nel Noddings, and Carolyn Mahar, 4:19–29. Journal for Research in Mathematics Education Monograph. Reston, VA: National Council of Teachers of Mathematics, 1990.

Glen, J. Stanley. *The Recovery of the Teaching Ministry*. Philadelphia, PA: Westminster Press, 1960.

Goheen, Michael W. "The Urgency of Reading the Bible as One Story." *Theology Today* 64, no. 4 (January 2008): 469–83.

Gower, Barry. *Scientific Method: A Historical and Philosophical Introduction.* Routledge, 2012.

Grabbe, Lester L. "The Hellenistic City of Jerusalem." In *Jews in the Hellenistic and Roman Cities*, edited by John R. Bartlett, 6–21. London and New York: Routledge, 2002.

Green, Steven K. *The Bible, the School, and the Constitution: The Clash That Shaped Modern Church-State Doctrine.* New York: Oxford University Press, 2012.

Gregg, Samuel. "Christians, Capitalism, and Culture: A Response to David Bentley Hart." *Public Discourse* (blog). Accessed December 11, 2015. http://www.thepublicdiscourse.com/2015/12/16117/.

Griffiths, Paul J. "The Vice of Curiosity." *Pro Ecclesia* 15, no. 1 (2006): 47–63.

Groome, Thomas H. *Will There Be Faith?: A New Vision for Educating and Growing Disciples.* New York: HarperOne, 2011.

Guenther, Bruce L. "The 'Enduring Problem' of Christ and Culture." *Direction Journal.* Accessed July 19, 2017. http://www.directionjournal.org/34/2/enduring-problem-of-christ-and-culture.html.

Gutek, Gerald L. *An Historical Introduction to American Education.* 3rd ed. Long Grove, IL: Waveland Press, 2012.

Hall, Stuart. "Encoding, Decoding." In *The Cultural Studies Reader*, edited by Simon During, 2nd ed., 90–103. London: Routledge, 1999.

Hall, Stuart, and Tony Jefferson, eds. *Resistance Through Rituals: Youth Subcultures in Post-War Britain.* 2nd rev. expanded ed. London and New York: Routledge, 2006.

Hamilton, David. "Instruction in the Making: Peter Ramus and the Beginnings of Modern Schooling." Presented at the American Educational Research Association annual meeting, Chicago, April 21, 2003.

———. *Towards a Theory of Schooling.* London: Falmer Press, 1989.

Harakas, Stanley Samuel. "Faith Formation in Byzantium." In *Educating People of Faith: Exploring the History of Jewish and Christian Communities*, edited by John H. Van Engen, 115–31. Grand Rapids, MI: Eerdmans, 2004.

Harland, Philip A. "The Declining Polis? Religious Rivalries in Ancient Civic Context." In *Religious Rivalries in the Early Roman Empire and the Rise of Christianity*, edited by Leif E. Vaage, 21–49. Vol. 18 of Studies in Christianity and Judaism. Waterloo, Ontario: Wilfrid Laurier University Press, 2006.

Harmless, William. *Augustine and the Catechumenate.* Collegeville, MN: Liturgical Press, 1995.

Harper, Kyle. *From Shame to Sin: The Christian Transformation of Sexual Morality in Late Antiquity.* Cambridge, MA: Harvard University Press, 2013.

Harrington, Austin. "Social Theory and Theology." In *The Handbook of Contemporary European Social Theory*, edited by Gerard Delanty, 37–47. Abingdon and New York: Routledge, 2006.

Hart, David Bentley. *Atheist Delusions: The Christian Revolution and Its Fashionable Enemies.* New Haven, CT: Yale University Press, 2009.

———. "Christ's Rabble." *Commonweal Magazine.* Accessed December 16, 2016. https://www.commonwealmagazine.org/christs-rabble.

Hatch, Edwin. *The Influence of Greek Ideas on Christianity*. London: Williams and Norgate, 1891.

Hawkins, Greg L., and Cally Parkinson. *Move: What 1,000 Churches Reveal about Spiritual Growth*. Grand Rapids, MI: Zondervan, 2011.

Heather, Peter John. *Empires and Barbarians: Migration, Development and the Birth of Europe*. London: Macmillan, 2009.

Hengel, Martin. *Judaism and Hellenism: Studies in Their Encounter in Palestine During the Early Hellenistic Period*. Translated by John Bowden. Philadelphia, PA: Fortress Press, 1981.

Hine, Iona. "The Quest for Biblical Literacy: Curricula, Culture, and Case Studies." In *Rethinking Biblical Literacy*, edited by Katie B. Edwards, 47–67. London: Bloomsbury Publishing, 2015.

Hock, Ronald F. "Paul and Greco-Roman Education." In *Paul in the Greco-Roman World: A Handbook*, edited by J. Paul Sampley, 198–227. Harrisburg, PA: Trinity Press International, 2003.

Hoek, Annewies van den. "The 'Catechetical' School of Early Christian Alexandria and Its Philonic Heritage." *Harvard Theological Review* 90, no. 1 (January 1997): 59–87.

Hogan, David. "The Market Revolution and Disciplinary Power: Joseph Lancaster and the Psychology of the Early Classroom System." *History of Education Quarterly* 29, no. 3 (1989): 381.

Horn, Cornelia B., and John W. Martens. *"Let the Little Children Come to Me": Childhood and Children in Early Christianity*. Washington, DC: CUA Press, 2009.

Horne, Herman H. *Jesus, the Master Teacher*. New York: Association Press, 1920.

Huebner, Dwayne. "Can Theological Education Be Church Education?" *Union Seminary Quarterly Review* 47 (1993): 23–38.

Hull, J. E. "Aiming for Christian Education, Settling for Christians Educating: The Christian School's Replication of a Public School Paradigm." *Christian Scholars Review* 32, no. 2 (2003): 203–24.

Huntington, Samuel P. "The Clash of Civilizations?" *Foreign Affairs* 72, no. 3 (Summer 1993): 22–49.

IJsseling, Samuel. *Rhetoric and Philosophy in Conflict: An Historical Survey*. Dordrecht and London: Springer, 1976.

Jackson, Philip W. *Life in Classrooms*. New York: Holt, Rinehart and Winston, 1968.

Jaeger, Werner. *Early Christianity and Greek Paideia*. Cambridge: Belknap Press, 1961.

Jenson, R. W. "How the World Lost Its Story." *First Things* 36 (1993): 19–24.

———. "On the Renewing of the Mind." In *Essays in Theology of Culture*, 163–74. Grand Rapids, MI: Eerdmans, 1995.

Johnson, Luke Timothy. *Living Jesus: Learning the Heart of the Gospel*. New York: HarperCollins, 2000.

Johnson, Maxwell E. *The Rites of Christian Initiation: Their Evolution and Interpretation*. Collegeville, MI: Liturgical Press, 2007.

Kaestle, Carl F. *Joseph Lancaster and the Monitorial School Movement: A Documentary History*. New York: Teachers College Press, 1973.

Kant, Immanuel. *Foundations of the Metaphysics of Morals and, What Is Enlightenment*. Macmillan, 1990.

Kidder, Paulette. "The Eclipse of Transcendence in Dickens' *Hard Times*." Presented at the Eric Voegelin Society (American Political Science Association), Chicago, September 2, 2004. http://www.lsu.edu/artsci/groups/voegelin/society/2004%20 Papers/Kidder2004.shtml.

———. "Martha Nussbaum on Dickens's *Hard Times*." *Philosophy and Literature* 33, no. 2 (2009): 417–26.

Kimball, Bruce A. *Orators and Philosophers: A History of the Idea of Liberal Education*. New York: Teachers College Press, 1986.

Kinnaman, David. *You Lost Me: Why Young Christians Are Leaving Church . . . and Rethinking Faith*. International ed. Grand Rapids, MI: Baker, 2011.

Kliebard, Herbert. "The Rise of the Scientific Curriculum and Its Aftermath." In *The Curriculum Studies Reader*, edited by David J. Flinders and Stephen J. Thornton, 37–46. New York: Routledge, 2004.

Knight, George R. "What Knowledge Is of Most Worth? Adventist Colleges and the Search for Meaning." *Journal of Adventist Education* 54 (1991): 5–8.

Kolodny, Niko. "The Explanation of Amour-Propre." *Philosophical Review* 119, no. 2 (April 1, 2010): 165–200.

Krathwohl, David R. "A Revision of Bloom's Taxonomy: An Overview." *Theory into Practice* 41, no. 4 (2002): 212–18.

Krathwohl, David R., Benjamin S. Bloom, and Bertram B. Masia. *Taxonomy of Educational Objectives: The Classification of Educational Goals, Handbook II: Affective Domain*. New York and London: Longman Group, 1964.

Kuhn, Thomas S. *The Structure of Scientific Revolutions: 50th Anniversary Edition*. Fourth ed. Chicago and London: University of Chicago Press, 2012.

Küng, Hans, and David Tracy. *Paradigm Change in Theology*. New York: Crossroad, 1989.

Kurian, George T. "Catechesis in the Early Church." Edited by George T. Kurian and Mark A. Lamport. *Encyclopedia of Christian Education*. Lanham, MD: Rowman & Littlefield, 2015.

Lake, Kirsopp. "The Apostles' Creed." *Harvard Theological Review* 17, no. 2 (1924): 173–183.

Lave, Jean. "A Comparative Approach to Educational Forms and Learning Processes." *Anthropology & Education Quarterly* 13, no. 2 (1982): 181–87.

———. "Situating Learning in Communities of Practice." In *Perspectives on Socially Shared Cognition*, 2:63–82, 1991.

Lave, Jean, and Etienne Wenger. *Situated Learning: Legitimate Peripheral Participation*. Cambridge and New York: Cambridge University Press, 1991.

Leach, A. F. *The Schools of Medieval England*. London: Methuen, 1915.

Lee, J. M. *The Shape of Religious Instruction: A Social-Science Approach*. Birmingham, AL: Religious Education Press, 1971.

Lewis, Robert. *Raising a Modern-Day Knight: A Father's Role in Guiding His Son to Authentic Manhood*. Carol Stream, IL: Tyndale, 2007.

Longo, Oddone. "Theatre of the Polis." In *Nothing to Do with Dionysos?: Athenian Drama in Its Social Context*, edited by John J. Winkler and Froma I. Zeitlin. Princeton, NJ: Princeton University Press, 1992.

Lynn, Robert W., and Elliott Wright. *The Big Little School: Sunday Child of American Protestantism*. New York: Harper & Row, 1971.

MacIntyre, Alasdair C. "Epistemological Crises, Dramatic Narrative, and the Philosophy of Science." In *Paradigms and Revolutions: Appraisals and Applications of Thomas Kuhn's Philosophy of Science*, edited by Gary Gutting, 54–74. South Bend, IN: University of Notre Dame Press, 1974.

Mackintosh, Robin. *Augustine of Canterbury: Leadership, Spirituality and Mission*. Norwich, UK: Canterbury Press, 2013.

"Mark Hopkins." *Britannica Online Encyclopedia*. Accessed May 19, 2017. https://www.britannica.com/print/article/271551.

Marquardt, Elizabeth, Charles E. Stokes, and Amy Zeittlow. "Does the Shape of Families Shape Faith?: Challenging the Churches to Confront the Impact of Family Change." In *Torn Asunder: Children, the Myth of the Good Divorce, and the Recovery of Origins*, edited by Margaret McCarthy, 66–90. Grand Rapids, MI: Eerdmans, 2017.

Marrou, H. I. *A History of Education in Antiquity*. Translated by G. Lamb. Madison and London: University of Wisconsin Press, 1982.

Martin, Jane Roland. "What Should We Do with a Hidden Curriculum When We Find One?" In *Changing the Educational Landscape: Philosophy, Women, and Curriculum*, 154–69. New York and London: Routledge, 1994.

Mayr-Harting, Henry. *Coming of Christianity to Anglo-Saxon England*. University Park, PA: Penn State Press, 2010.

Mazza, Enrico. *Mystagogy: A Theology of Liturgy in the Patristic Age*. Liturgical Press, 1989.

McCarthy, Daryll. "Hearts and Minds Aflame for Christ: Irish Monks—a Model for Academic Missions." Grand Rapids, MI: 2001.

McCrindle, Mark. "A Demographic Snapshot of Christianity and Church Attenders in Australia." Bella Vista, NSW, Australia: McCrindle Research, April 18, 2014.

McLaren, Peter. *Schooling as a Ritual Performance: Toward a Political Economy of Educational Symbols and Gestures*. Lanham, MD: Rowman & Littlefield, 1999.

McNair, Chris. *Young Lions: Christian Rites of Passage for African-American Young Men*. Nashville, TN: Abingdon Press, 2001.

Milbank, John. *Theology and Social Theory: Beyond Secular Reason*. 2nd ed. Malden, MA and Oxford: Blackwell Publisher, 2006.

Moran, Jo Ann Hoeppner. *The Growth of English Schooling, 1340–1548: Learning, Literacy, and Laicization in Pre-Reformation York Diocese*. Princeton Legacy Library. Princeton, NJ: Princeton University Press, 2014.

Morgan, Donn F. "Education." Edited by David Noel Freedman, Astrid B. Beck, and Allen C. Myers. *Eerdmans Dictionary of the Bible*. Grand Rapids, MI: Eerdmans, 2000.

Morgan, Edward. *The Incarnation of the Word: The Theology of Language of Augustine of Hippo*. London and New York: T & T Clark, 2010.

Morley, Patrick. *The Young Man in the Mirror: A Rite of Passage into Manhood*. Nashville, TN: B&H, 2003.

Morrison, Philip E. "Implications of Paul's Model for Leadership Training in Light of Church Growth in Africa." *Africa Journal of Evangelical Theology* 30 (2011): 56.

Murphy, Debra Dean. *Teaching That Transforms: Worship as the Heart of Christian Education*. Eugene, OR: Wipf and Stock, 2007.

Murray, Stuart. *Church Planting: Laying Foundations*. Scottdale, PA: Herald Press, 2001.

Naugle, David K. *Worldview: The History of a Concept*. Grand Rapids, MI: Eerdmans, 2002.

Newbigin, Lesslie. *The Gospel in a Pluralist Society*. Grand Rapids, MI: Eerdmans, 1989.

Newell, Edward J. *"Education Has Nothing to Do with Theology": James Michael Lee's Social Science Religious Instruction*. Vol. 61 of Princeton Theological Monograph Series. Eugene, OR: Pickwick Publications, 2006.

Newell, Ted. "Worldviews in Collision: Jesus as Critical Educator." *Journal of Education & Christian Belief* 13, no. 2 (2009): 141–54.

Neyrey, Jerome H. "The Social Location of Paul: Education as the Key." *Fabrics of Discourse: Essays in Honor of Vernon K. Robbins*, 2003, 126–64.

Niebuhr, H. Richard. *Christ and Culture*. Harper & Row, 1975.

Nord, W. A. *Does God Make a Difference?: Taking Religion Seriously in Our Schools and Universities*. New York: Oxford University Press, 2010.

Nord, Warren A. *Religion and American Education: Rethinking a National Dilemma*. Chapel Hill: UNC Press Books, 1995.

Ong, Walter J. *Ramus, Method, and the Decay of Dialogue: From the Art of Discourse to the Art of Reason*. Chicago: University of Chicago Press, 2005.

Orme, Nicholas. "For Richer, For Poorer?: Free Education in England, c.1380–1530." *The Journal of the History of Childhood and Youth* 1, no. 2 (May 25, 2008): 169–87.

———. *Medieval Schools: From Roman Britain to Renaissance England*. New Haven, CT: Yale University Press, 2006.

Osmer, R. R., and F. Schweitzer. *Religious Education between Modernization and Globalization: New Perspectives on the United States and Germany*. Grand Rapids, MI: Eerdmans, 2003.

Osmer, Richard R. "Practical Theology: A Current International Perspective." *HTS Teologiese Studies / Theological Studies* 67, no. 2 (November 16, 2011): 1–7.

Palmer, Parker J. *The Courage to Teach: Exploring the Inner Landscape of a Teacher's Life*. 1st ed. San Francisco: Jossey-Bass, 1997.

Parker, Robert. "Greek Religion." In *The Oxford History of the Classical World*, edited by John Boardman, Jasper Griffin, and Oswyn Murray. Oxford: Oxford University Press, 1986.

Parrett, Gary, and J. I. Packer. *Grounded in the Gospel: Building Believers the Old-Fashioned Way*. Grand Rapids, MI: Baker, 2010.

Passmore, John Arthur. *The Perfectibility of Man*. 3rd ed. Indianapolis: Liberty Foundation, 2000.

Paul, Richard W. "Bloom's Taxonomy and Critical Thinking Instruction." *Educational Leadership* 42, no. 8 (1985): 36–39.

Penner, James, R. Harder, R. Hiemstra, E. Anderson, and B. Désorcy. "Hemorrhaging Faith: Why and When Canadian Young Adults Are Leaving, Staying and Returning to Church." Foundational Research Document Commissioned by EFC Youth and Young Adult Ministry Roundtable. Ottawa: Evangelical Fellowship of Canada, 2012.

Perkins, Pheme. *Jesus as Teacher*. Cambridge: Cambridge University Press, 1990.

Petersen, Joan. "The Education of Girls in Fourth-Century Rome." In *Christianity and Society: The Social World of Early Christianity*, edited by Everett Ferguson, 77–86. New York and London: Garland Publishing, 1999.

Petrina, Stephen, Franc Feng, and Yu-Ling Lee. "On the Historiography of Curriculum: The Legend of Petrus Ramus." Washington, DC, 2016.

Phillips, D. C., and Jonas F. Soltis. *Perspectives on Learning*. 5th ed. New York: Teachers College Press, 2009.

Plato. *Plato's Symposium*. Translated by Seth Benardete. Chicago: University of Chicago Press, 1993.

Polanyi, Michael. *Personal Knowledge: Towards a Post-Critical Philosophy*. Chicago: University of Chicago Press, 1958.

———. *The Tacit Dimension*. Chicago: University of Chicago Press, 2009.

Pollatschek, Nele. "'Discard the Word Fancy Altogether!' Charles Dickens's Defense of Ambiguity in Hard Times." *Dickens Quarterly* 30, no. 4 (December 1, 2013): 278.

Redford, Jeremy, Danielle Battle, and Stacey Bielick. "Homeschooling in the United States: 2012," 2016. https://eric.ed.gov/?id=ED569947.

Rees, Jonathan. "Frederick Taylor in the Classroom: Standardized Testing and Scientific Management." *Radical Pedagogy* 10 (2001).

Reigart, John Franklin. *The Lancasterian System of Instruction in the Schools of New York City*. New York: Teachers College, Columbia University, 1916.

Rieff, Philip. *The Triumph of the Therapeutic: Uses of Faith after Freud*. Chicago: University of Chicago Press, 1987.

Riley, Naomi Schaefer. "From Generation to Generation." *Wall Street Journal—Eastern Edition* 263, no. 21 (January 27, 2014): A11.

Rousseau, J. J. *Émile, or On Education*. Translated by Allan Bloom. New York: Basic Books, 1979.

Ruden, Sarah. *Paul among the People: The Apostle Reinterpreted and Reimagined in His Own Time*. New York: Image Books, 2010.

Sammons, Jack. "Parables and Pedagogy." In *Gladly Learn, Gladly Teach: Living Out One's Calling in the Twenty-First Century Academy*, edited by J. M. Dunaway, 46–66. Macon, GA: Mercer University Press, 2005.

Schön, Donald A. *The Reflective Practitioner: How Professionals Think in Action*. New York: Basic Books, 1983.

Setran, David P., and Chris A. Kiesling. *Spiritual Formation in Emerging Adulthood: A Practical Theology for College and Young Adult Ministry*. Grand Rapids, MI: Baker Academic, 2013.

Silber, Kate. *Pestalozzi: The Man and His Work*. New York: Schocken Books, 1973.

Skelton, Alan. "Studying Hidden Curricula: Developing a Perspective in the Light of Postmodern Insights." *Curriculum Studies* 5, no. 2 (1997): 177–93.

Sloan, Douglas. *Faith and Knowledge: Mainline Protestantism and American Higher Education*. Louisville, KY: Westminster / John Knox Press, 1994.

Smith, Christian, and Melinda Lundquist Denton. *Soul Searching: The Religious and Spiritual Lives of American Teenagers*. New York: Oxford University Press US, 2005.

Smith, Christian, and Patricia Snell. *Souls in Transition: The Religious and Spiritual Lives of Emerging Adults*. New York: Oxford University Press, 2009.

Smith, David I., and Barbara Maria Carvill. *The Gift of the Stranger: Faith, Hospitality, and Foreign Language Learning*. Grand Rapids, MI: Eerdmans, 2000.

Smith, David I., and Susan M. Felch. *Teaching and Christian Imagination*. Grand Rapids, MI: Eerdmans, 2015.

Smith, David I., and James K. A. Smith. *Teaching and Christian Practices: Reshaping Faith and Learning*. Grand Rapids, MI: Eerdmans, 2011.

Smith, James K. A. *Desiring the Kingdom: Worship, Worldview, and Cultural Formation*. Cultural Liturgies. Grand Rapids, MI: Baker Academic, 2009.

Smith, M. K. "Johann Heinrich Pestalozzi: Pedagogy, Education and Social Justice." *Infed.Org* (blog), 2014. http://infed.org/mobi/johann-heinrich-pestalozzi-pedagogy-education-and-social-justice/.

Spears, P. D., and S. R. Loomis. *Education for Human Flourishing: A Christian Perspective*. Downers Grove, IL: IVP Academic, 2009.

Spencer, Herbert. "What Knowledge Is of Most Worth?" In *Education: Intellectual, Moral, and Physical*, 5–92. New York: Hurst and Company, 1862.

Steeg, Susanna M. "Families and Faith: How Religion Is Passed Down across Generations." *International Journal of Christianity & Education* 19, no. 1 (March 1, 2015): 77–78.

Steudeman, Michael J. "Horace Mann, 'The Necessity of Education in a Republican Government' (Fall 1839)." *Voices of Democracy* 8 (2013): 1–22.

Strathmann, H. "Polis." Edited by Gerhard Kittel and Gerhard Friedrich. Translated by Geoffrey William Bromiley. *Theological Dictionary of the New Testament*. Grand Rapids, MI: Eerdmans, 1990.

Strauss, Gerald. "The Social Function of Schools in the Lutheran Reformation in Germany." *History of Education Quarterly* 28, no. 2 (1988): 191.

Stronks, Gloria G., and Doug Blomberg, eds. *A Vision with a Task: Christian Schooling for Responsive Discipleship*. Grand Rapids, MI: Baker, 1993.

Swancutt, Diana. "Scripture 'Reading' and Identity Formation in Paul: Paideia among Believing Greeks." Washington, DC, 2006.

Thompson, Glen. "Teaching the Teachers: Pastoral Education in the Early Church." *Wisconsin Lutheran Quarterly* 94, no. 2 (1997): 103–14.

Tolbert, Mary Ann. "How the Gospel of Mark Builds Character." *Interpretation: A Journal of Bible & Theology* 47, no. 4 (October 1993): 347.

Tyack, David B. *The One Best System: A History of American Urban Education*. Cambridge, MA: Harvard University Press, 1974.

Tyler, Ralph W. "The Five Most Significant Curriculum Events in the Twentieth Century." *Educational Leadership* 44, no. 4 (1987): 36–8.

Van Brummelen, Harro W. *Walking with God in the Classroom.* Colorado Springs: Purposeful Design, 2009.

Van Manen, Max. "On the Epistemology of Reflective Practice." *Teachers and Teaching: Theory and Practice* 1, no. 1 (1995): 33–50.

———. "Pedagogy, Virtue, and Narrative Identity in Teaching." *Curriculum Inquiry* 24, no. 2 (1994): 135–70.

Vaughan, Michalina, and Margaret Scotford Archer. *Social Conflict and Educational Change in England and France 1789–1848.* Cambridge: Cambridge University Press, 2010.

Voas, David. "The Rise and Fall of Fuzzy Fidelity in Europe." *European Sociological Review* 25, no. 2 (2009): 155–68.

Voas, David, and Mark Chaves. "Is the United States a Counterexample to the Secularization Thesis?" *American Journal of Sociology* 121, no. 5 (March 2016): 1517–56.

Voas, David, and Alasdair Crockett. "Religion in Britain: Neither Believing nor Belonging." *Sociology* 39, no. 1 (February 2005): 11–28.

Voas, David, and Stefanie Doebler. "Secularization in Europe: Religious Change Between and Within Birth Cohorts." *Religion and Society in Central and Eastern Europe* 4, no. 1 (2011): 39–62.

Wach, Joachim. "Master and Disciple: Two Religio-Sociological Studies." *The Journal of Religion* 42, no. 1 (1962): 1–21.

Walch, Timothy. *Parish School: American Catholic Parochial Education from Colonial Times to the Present.* Crossroad, 1996.

Walsh, Brian J. "Transformation: Dynamic Worldview or Repressive Ideology?" *Journal of Education and Christian Belief* 4, no. 2 (2000): 101–14.

Ward, Sir Adolphus William, and Alfred Rayney Waller, eds. "Education, § 17: Bell and Lancaster." In *The Victorian Age, Part Two.* Vol. XIV of The Cambridge History of English and American Literature in 18 Volumes (1907–21). London: Macmillan, 1933.

Warnick, Bryan R. "How Do We Learn from the Lives of Others?" *Philosophy of Education Archive*, 2006, 367–75.

Warren, Michael. "Religious Formation in the Context of Social Formation." In *Critical Perspectives on Christian Education: A Reader on the Aims, Principles and Philosophy of Christian Education*, edited by Jeff Astley and Leslie J. Francis, 202–14. Leominster, UK: Gracewing, 1994.

Wayman, Benjamin D. "Julian against Christian Educators: Julian and Basil on a Proper Education." *Christian Scholar's Review* 45, no. 3 (Spring 2016): 249–67.

Westerhoff, John H. *Will Our Children Have Faith?* Revised ed. Harrisburg, PA: Morehouse, 2000.

Wilhoit, James. "The Bible Goes to Sunday School: An Historical Response to Pluralism." *Religious Education* 82, no. 3 (1987): 390–404.

Williams, Raymond. *The Long Revolution.* London: Chatto & Windus, 1961.

Willigenburg, Stephanie van, and C. Marshall. "Judging Athenian Dramatic Competitions." *Journal of Hellenic Studies* 124 (2004): 90–107.

Wink, Walter. "The Education of the Apostles: Mark's View of Human Transformation." *Religious Education* 83, no. 2 (1988): 277–90.

Wolterstorff, Nicholas, Gloria G. Stronks, and Clarence Joldersma. *Educating for Life: Reflections on Christian Teaching and Learning*. Grand Rapids, MI: Baker Academic, 2002.

Worley, Robert C. *Preaching and Teaching in the Earliest Church*. Philadelphia, PA: Westminster Press, 1967.

Wright, Andrew. *Religious Education and Postmodernity*. London: RoutledgeFalmer, 2003.

Wright, N. T. "How Can the Bible Be Authoritative?" *Vox Evangelica* 21, no. 1991 (1991): 7–32.

———. *The New Testament and the People of God*. Vol. 1 of Christian Origins and the Question of God. London and Minneapolis: SPCK and Fortress, 1992.

Zauzmer, Julie. "How Decades of Divorce Helped Erode Religion." *Washington Post*, September 27, 2016, sec. Acts of Faith. https://www.washingtonpost.com/news/acts-of-faith/wp/2016/09/27/how-decades-of-divorce-helped-erode-religion/.

Zuck, R. B. *Teaching as Jesus Taught*. Grand Rapids, MI: Baker, 1995.

GENERAL INDEX

95 Theses, 87

Abelard, Pierre, 68–69, 132
Abraham, 38, 47
abstraction: of education, 51, 61, 64–65, 69, 72, 85, 93, 102, 116, 128; of knowledge, 64, 93, 128; of theology, 72, 114
Adam, 36, 49
Adamson, J. W., 60n8, 61n10, 65n17, 68n22, 73n28, 137
adherence, 16–17, 21, 29, 118–19, 122; *see also* church, attendance in
adolescence, 99–100. *See also* teenagers
Alcuin, 59, 66, 126, 131
Alexander the Great, 41
Alexandria, 46, 52
Alpha movement, 124
amor sciendi, 62
Anglican, 121
anthropology, 24, 26, 51, 125, 133
Aquinas, Thomas, 10, 111
Aratus, 43
architecture, 41, 43
Areopagus, 43
Aristophanes, 41
Aristotle, 41, 68, 71, 131
Ars Minor, 64
art, study of, 9, 19, 42–43, 68, 85, 120–21
asceticism, 59, 62. *See also* cloisters
Association for Biblical Higher Education, 113
Athens, 43, 47, 52n23
attendance: church, 16, 117–20, 144; school, 86, 88, 103, 120
Auerbach, Erich, 45n10, 137
Augustine: of Canterbury, 59–60, 131; of Hippo, 10, 45n10, 47–48, 54n28, 59, 62–65, 131
authority: of the Bible, 45, 47n13, 68–69, 150; of the church, 24, 69; of curriculum, 43, 68–70, 76n3, 80, 109, 115; of God, 113; of Jesus, 33; of

schools, 23–24, 68–69, 109, 113, 115; of thought, 69, 109
Ayres, Leonard, 86

Bach, Johann Sebastian, 10
bachelor's degree, 70
Baden-Powell, Robert, 119
baptism, 46, 52–54, 62, 119
Bayly, Joseph, 92n28, 138
Bell, Andrew, 81–82, 149
Benedict's rule, 59
Bentham, Jeremy, 82, 132, 135
Bible, the: authority of, 47n13, 150; and culture, 9, 124; in curriculum, 9, 60–61, 64, 67, 91, 113, 142; interpretation of, 9–10, 29, 39, 47, 61, 65, 91, 102, 113, 115; Old Testament, 18, 31, 36, 44–45, 47, 52; story of the, 47n13, 125, 141; study of the, 9, 13, 51, 60–67, 89, 115, 141; teaching the, 9, 13, 16, 44–47, 51, 57–73, 89, 106–7, 115
bildung, 17
Bloom, Benjamin, 57n3, 84–85, 129, 132, 139, 140, 144, 147
Bobbitt, Franklin, 83–84, 132, 133, 140
Boethius, 68
Bonaventure, 65, 132
Bosch, David, 26, 27n18, 137
Boy Scouts, 21, 119
Boys, Mary, 26, 27n18, 137
Brahe, Tycho, 77
Buddhism, 90, 109

Caesar, 45
Callahan, Raymond, 86–87, 138, 139
Calvinism, 88–89
Calvin, John, 56, 139
Cambridge University, 69–70, 139
Canada, 16, 24, 90, 113
Carr, Wilfred, 112, 139
Carver, George Washington, 10
Cassian, John, 47, 131
catechism, 46, 54–55, 63n15, 115–16, 124–25, 137, 143
cathedral school, 59–60, 69, 71, 120

SCRIPTURE INDEX

RECLAIMING THE
CHRISTIAN INTELLECTUAL TRADITION SERIES

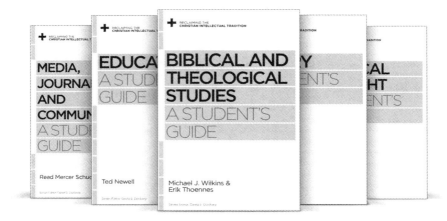

MEDIA, JOURNAL AND COMMUN A STUDY GUIDE

Read Mercer Schud

EDUCA A STUDE GUIDE

Ted Newell

BIBLICAL AND THEOLOGICAL STUDIES A STUDENT'S GUIDE

Michael J. Wilkins & Erik Thoennes

———— Series Volumes ————

- Biblical and Theological Studies
- Education
- Christian Worldview
- Philosophy
- The Great Tradition of Christian Thinking
- Ethics and Moral Reasoning
- The Liberal Arts

- Political Thought
- Literature
- Art and Music
- The Natural Sciences
- Psychology
- History
- Media, Journalism, and Communication

For more information, visit **crossway.org**.